Southern Living®
ALL-TIME FAVORITE
COOKIE
RECIPES

Southern Living®

ALL-TIME FAVORITE

COOKIE RECIPES

Compiled and Edited by
Jean Wickstrom Liles

Oxmoor
House®

Copyright 1995 by Oxmoor House, Inc.
Book Division of Southern Progress Corporation
P.O. Box 2465, Birmingham, Alabama 35201

Library of Congress Catalog Number: 95-74598
ISBN: 0-8487-2222-1
Manufactured in the United States of America
Second Printing 2003

Editor-in-Chief: Nancy Fitzpatrick Wyatt
Editorial Director, Special Interest Publications: Ann H. Harvey
Senior Foods Editor: Susan Carlisle Payne
Senior Editor, Editorial Services: Olivia Kindig Wells
Art Director: James Boone

Southern Living® ALL-TIME FAVORITE COOKIE RECIPES

Menu and Recipe Consultant: Jean Wickstrom Liles
Assistant Editor: Kelly Hooper Troiano
Copy Editor: Jane Phares
Editorial Assistants: Keri Bradford Anderson, Valorie J. Cooper
Indexer: Mary Ann Laurens
Concept Designer: Melissa Jones Clark
Designer: Rita Yerby
Senior Photographers: Jim Bathie; Charles Walton IV, *Southern Living* magazine
Photographers: Ralph Anderson; Tina Evans, J. Savage Gibson, Sylvia Martin, *Southern Living* magazine
Senior Photo Stylists: Kay E. Clarke; Leslie Byars Simpson, *Southern Living* magazine
Photo Stylists: Virginia R. Cravens; Ashley J. Wyatt, *Southern Living* magazine
Production and Distribution Director: Phillip Lee
Production Manager: Gail Morris
Associate Production and Distribution Manager: John Charles Gardner
Associate Production Manager: Theresa L. Beste
Production Assistant: Marianne Jordan Wilson

Our appreciation to the editorial staff of *Southern Living* magazine for their contributions to this volume.

Cover (*from top*): Almond Cream Squares (page 99), Old-Fashioned Peanut Butter Cookies (page 17),
    Cherry Crowns (page 132), Peppermint Patties (page 118), and Loaded-with-Chips Cookies (page 44)
Page 1: Triple Chip Cookies (page 46)
Page 2 (*clockwise from bottom right*): Date Pinwheel Cookies (page 69), Melt-Away Butter Cookies (page 34),
    Dainty Sandwich Cookies (page 77), Gingersnaps (page 14), and Easy Frosted Brownies (page 85)

Contents

All about Cookies

Cookies are special. Whether chock full of chocolate morsels, filled with jam, or cut into fancy shapes—cookies are irresistible, and there never seems to be enough of them. To help keep your cookie jar filled, try our baking hints for these sweet treats.

The Right Equipment

• Have several sturdy cookie sheets if you plan to bake a lot of cookies.

• Use shiny cookie sheets that are at least 2 inches narrower and shorter than your oven to allow heat to circulate evenly around them.

• Don't use pans with high sides for baking cookies, as they deflect the heat, causing the cookies to bake unevenly.

• If you have cookie sheets with a nonstick coating, watch the cookies carefully as they bake; dark-surfaced pans of this type tend to make cookies brown more quickly.

• Insulated cookie sheets—two sheets of aluminum with an air pocket sealed between them—are great for soft cookies and meringues, but cookies won't get crisp when baked on them.

• If your cookie sheets are thin and lightweight, place one on top of the other to prevent cookies from burning.

• Have a timer, a couple of wire cooling racks, and a sturdy spatula to remove cookies from cookie sheet to wire rack to cool.

Cookie Baking Tips

• Regular butter and margarine can be used interchangeably in most cookie recipes. However, it is not wise to substitute whipped butter, whipped margarine, or reduced-calorie margarine when baking. Additional air in whipped products and a higher water content in reduced-calorie margarine may break down during baking, resulting in thin, flat cookies.

• Brown sugar should be firmly packed into a measuring cup so that it holds its shape when turned out. Break up any lumps, or they will melt during baking, creating holes in the baked cookies.

• All-purpose flour is sifted before packaging. Just spoon flour into a measuring cup, and level with a flat edge.

• Stir dry ingredients together before adding to mix to ensure that the leavening agents will be evenly distributed.

• To prevent stiff cookie dough from straining hand-held portable mixers, stir in the last additions of flour mixture by hand.

• Keep mixing to a minimum once the flour has been added; overmixing produces tough cookies.

• Preheat oven 10 minutes before baking cookies.

• Grease the cookie sheet only if directed in the recipe, using vegetable cooking spray or solid shortening (not butter or margarine).

• Place cookies at least 2 inches apart on shiny, heavy aluminum cookie sheets. Sheets that have darkened may absorb heat, causing the cookie bottoms to become overly brown.

• To bake cookies all the same size, spoon dough in equal amounts onto cookie sheet.

• Bake one cookie sheet at a time on the middle oven rack; if you need to bake more than one, rotate the sheets from the top to the bottom rack halfway through baking time.

• Keep an eye on the first batch placed in the oven; check for doneness at the minimum baking time or 2 to 3 minutes before the amount of time indicated in the recipe.

• Transfer baked cookies to a wire rack immediately after baking unless otherwise directed. (Delicate cookies must cool slightly on the cookie sheet to become firm enough to transfer.) If cookies remain on the cookie sheet too long, they may stick; to loosen cookies, return cookie sheet to oven for 1 minute.

• Allow cookie sheets to cool before reusing; wipe surface with a paper towel, or scrape off crumbs to prevent next batch from sticking.

Making Great Cookies

Cookies come in a wide array of types and shapes. For convenience, most of the cookies in this book are organized by cookie-making techniques. But the last chapter spotlights holiday cookies of many flavors, styles, and shapes.

Shaped Cookies

• Dough for these cookies is formed by hand into a variety of designs or transformed into shapes using a cookie press, molds, rosette iron, or even a waffle iron.

• Cookies shaped by hand are usually baked as balls or shaped into more intricate designs (wreaths, crescents, or pretzels).

• If dough seems too soft to shape, chill until it's firm enough to shape. If still too soft, mix in 1 to 2 tablespoons flour.

• When making pressed cookies, test dough for consistency before adding all the flour. Put a small amount of dough in cookie press and make a sample cookie. Dough should be pliable but not crumbly.

• When shaping dough into balls, roll balls the same size so cookies will be uniform after baking. Some cookies retain their shape during baking while others flatten slightly and look crinkly on top.

• For a sugary appearance and taste, roll balls of dough in sugar before baking.

Drop Cookies

• Dough for these cookies is literally dropped from two spoons (not measuring spoons) onto cookie sheets with no further shaping necessary. Or save time by dropping dough using a small, all-purpose scoop.

• Excessive spreading may be caused if the cookie sheet is too hot, oven temperature is incorrect, or dough is too warm. Chilling the dough helps prevent this.

• Allow at least 2 inches between cookies on the cookie sheet.

Refrigerated Cookies

• These cookies are classified as make-ahead cookies because the dough needs to be thoroughly chilled.

• Dough for sliced or refrigerator cookies is shaped into a log and chilled until firm enough to slice easily.

• For slice-and-bake cookies, chill the dough up to 7 days. Slice the dough, and bake only the number of cookies you want.

• When cutting a log of chilled dough, give the log a quarter turn every 5 slices to keep it round.

• For rolled cookies, shape dough into a ball and chill.

• When ready to bake, divide dough into 2 or 3 equal portions. Roll 1 portion of dough at a time and keep the rest chilled. Excessive rolling causes tough cookies.

• Dough for rolled cookies is stiff enough to be rolled to a designated thickness and cut with cookie cutters. To prevent dough from sticking, roll dough on a lightly floured surface or pastry cloth, or use a stockinette cover on your rolling pin.

• If dough seems too soft to roll after chilling, roll it onto the cookie sheet. Cut with cookie cutters and peel away the scraps. This saves time and speeds cleanup.

• When rolling dough, start at the center and roll outward.

• For easy cleanup, roll dough on a wax paper-covered surface. To keep the wax paper from slipping, sprinkle a few drops of water on surface before arranging the wax paper.

• Dip cookie cutter in flour or powdered sugar to keep dough from sticking.

Decorating Cutout Cookies

• Washable pastry bags and metal pastry tips are handy when piping frosting. Fill bags no more than two-thirds full, and twist the upper third tightly to prevent the frosting from coming out the top as you pipe it through the tip.

• Disposable pastry bags are also available, or make your own by rolling triangles of parchment paper into cones.

Bars and Squares

• This unbaked dough is usually stiff and is baked in a pan. Cool completely in pan before cutting into bars, squares, or diamonds.

• Use the size of pan called for in the recipe. Altering the pan size will affect the baking time and texture of the cookie.

• Overmixing bar cookies results in a hard and crusty top; overbaking makes a dry and crumbly cookie.

• Try lining the baking dish with a large piece of aluminum foil. This will make it easy to remove baked brownies or bar cookies from the pan.

• For a quick glaze on bar cookies, sprinkle the surface with chocolate morsels after removing cookies from oven. Cover with foil, and let stand 3 to 5 minutes or until chocolate melts. Spread chocolate evenly over surface.

Keeping Cookies on Hand

Cookies are among the very easiest sweet treats to store. If you follow the suggestions below, cookies and bars will maintain their fresh taste and appearance for several days, or, if frozen, up to 8 months.

Storing Cookies

• Let cookies cool completely before storing.

• Avoid storing soft cookies and crisp cookies in the same container, or the crisp cookies will become soft.

• Store soft, chewy cookies in an airtight container along with a slice of apple to maintain moisture. Remove the apple after 1 or 2 days. This technique also works with soft cookies that are dry because of overbaking or age.

• Place crisp cookies in a container with a loose-fitting lid. If they soften, recrisp by heating at 300° for 3 to 5 minutes.

• Store bar cookies in the pan in which they were baked. Seal tightly with plastic wrap or aluminum foil.

• Separate layers of decorated or moist cookies with wax paper to prevent their sticking together.

Freezing Cookies

• Most cookie dough can be tightly wrapped and frozen up to 6 months before baking.

• Thaw cookie dough in the refrigerator or at room temperature until it's a good consistency to shape as the recipe directs. For slice-and-bake cookies, slice frozen dough with a sharp knife.

• Unfrosted cookies freeze well for 8 months. Package them in an airtight container with plastic wrap or wax paper between layers, crumpling extra plastic wrap or wax paper to fill any air spaces. Label and freeze.

• Frosted cookies can be frozen 2 to 3 months. Freeze them uncovered until firm; then pack in a single layer in an airtight container.

• Thaw baked cookies in container about 15 minutes at room temperature.

Shapes of All Varieties

From old-fashioned molasses cookies to an assortment of dainty delights, these flavorful treats allow you to become a creative artist. Plain or fancy, one thing is certain—they're all delicious.

Almond Cookies, Brown Sugar-Pecan Cookies, Walnut Cookies

Mocha Surprise Truffles, Surprise Bonbon Cookies, Chocolate-Tipped Butter Cookies

Crispy Coconut-Oatmeal Cookies, Chocolate-Ginger Crinkles, Almond Spritz Cookies

Chocolate Waffle Cookies, Buttery Lace Cookies, Delicate Madeleines

Old-Fashioned Peanut Butter Cookies (page 17)

Almond Cookies

⅔ cup shortening
1⅔ cups sugar
2 large eggs
1 teaspoon almond extract
2½ cups all-purpose flour
2 teaspoons baking powder
½ teaspoon baking soda
¼ teaspoon salt
1 egg white, slightly beaten
About ¼ cup sliced almonds

Beat shortening at medium speed of an electric mixer until fluffy; gradually add sugar, beating well. Add eggs and almond extract, beating well. Combine flour, baking powder, soda, and salt; stir into creamed mixture.

Shape dough into 1½-inch balls; flatten slightly. Brush with beaten egg white. Place 3 sliced almonds in center of each cookie.

Bake at 375° for 15 minutes or until lightly browned. Cool on wire racks. **Yield: about 3 dozen.**

Texan-Size Almond Crunch Cookies

1 cup sugar
1 cup sifted powdered sugar
1 cup butter or margarine, softened
1 cup vegetable oil
2 large eggs
2 teaspoons almond extract
3½ cups all-purpose flour
1 cup whole wheat flour
1 teaspoon baking soda
1 teaspoon salt
1 teaspoon cream of tartar
2 cups chopped almonds
1 (6-ounce) package almond brickle chips
Sugar

Combine first 4 ingredients in a large mixing bowl; beat at medium speed of an electric mixer until blended. Add eggs and almond extract, beating well.

Combine flours, soda, salt, and cream of tartar; gradually add to creamed mixture, beating

Brown Sugar-Pecan Cookies and Texan-Size Almond Crunch Cookies

just until blended after each addition. Stir in almonds and brickle chips. Cover and chill 3 to 4 hours.

Shape dough into 1½-inch balls, and place at least 3 inches apart on ungreased cookie sheets. Flatten cookies with a fork dipped in sugar, making a crisscross pattern.

Bake at 350° for 14 to 15 minutes or until lightly browned. Transfer to wire racks to cool. **Yield: about 4 dozen.**

Brown Sugar-Pecan Cookies

1 cup butter or margarine, softened
½ cup firmly packed brown sugar
½ cup sugar
1 large egg
1 teaspoon vanilla extract
2 cups all-purpose flour
½ teaspoon baking soda
¼ teaspoon salt
½ cup finely chopped pecans
Brown Sugar Frosting
Pecan halves

Beat butter at medium speed of an electric mixer until creamy; gradually add sugars, mixing well. Add egg and vanilla; beat well.

Combine flour, soda, and salt; gradually add to creamed mixture, mixing well after each addition. Stir in chopped pecans. Cover and chill 30 minutes.

Shape dough into 1-inch balls; place on ungreased cookie sheets. Bake at 350° for 10 to 12 minutes. Cool on wire racks, and spread Brown Sugar Frosting over tops. Top each cookie with a pecan half. **Yield: 5 dozen.**

Brown Sugar Frosting

1 cup firmly packed brown sugar
½ cup half-and-half
1 tablespoon butter or margarine
1½ to 1⅔ cups sifted powdered sugar

Combine brown sugar and half-and-half in a saucepan. Cook over medium heat, stirring constantly, until mixture comes to a boil; boil 4 minutes. Remove from heat. Stir in butter.

Add 1½ cups powdered sugar, and beat at medium speed of an electric mixer until smooth. Gradually add remaining powdered sugar to desired spreading consistency. **Yield: 1⅓ cups.**

Pecan-Butter Cookies

1 cup butter or margarine, softened
1 cup sugar
2 egg yolks
¾ teaspoon vanilla extract
¾ teaspoon almond extract
½ teaspoon lemon extract
2 cups all-purpose flour
1 teaspoon baking powder
¼ teaspoon salt
About 1 cup pecan halves

Beat butter at medium speed of an electric mixer until creamy; gradually add sugar, beating well. Add egg yolks, one at a time, beating until blended after each addition. Stir in flavorings.

Combine flour, baking powder, and salt. Add to creamed mixture, and beat well.

Roll dough into 1-inch balls; place about 2 inches apart on ungreased cookie sheets. Press a pecan half into center of each cookie.

Bake at 300° for 20 minutes or until lightly browned. Cool on wire racks. **Yield: about 3½ dozen.**

Cookie Tip

Use a fork to flatten balls of cookie dough in a criss-cross pattern. Dip the tines of the fork in sugar or flour so that the dough will not stick.

Hazelnut Cookies

1 cup butter or margarine, softened
½ cup sifted powdered sugar
2 cups all-purpose flour
1 cup finely chopped hazelnuts, toasted
Sifted powdered sugar

   Beat butter at medium speed of an electric mixer until creamy. Add ½ cup sugar; beat until light and fluffy. Gradually add flour; beat well. Stir in hazelnuts. Cover and chill 30 minutes.
   Shape dough into 1-inch balls; place on ungreased cookie sheets. Bake at 400° for 12 to 14 minutes. Remove immediately from cookie sheets; roll in powdered sugar. **Yield: 3½ dozen.**

Easy Walnut Cookies

½ cup butter or margarine, softened
2 tablespoons sugar
1 cup all-purpose flour
1 teaspoon walnut extract
1 cup walnuts, finely chopped
¾ cup sifted powdered sugar

   Beat butter and 2 tablespoons sugar at medium speed of an electric mixer until blended. Stir in flour. Add walnut extract and walnuts, stirring well. Cover and chill 30 minutes.
   Shape dough into 1-inch balls; place on ungreased cookie sheet. Bake at 350° for 15 minutes. Roll in powdered sugar. **Yield: 2½ dozen.**

Walnut Cookies

½ cup butter or margarine, softened
½ cup sugar
1 large egg, separated
¾ teaspoon grated lemon rind
1 cup all-purpose flour
¼ teaspoon salt
¼ teaspoon ground cinnamon
⅛ teaspoon ground cloves
1¾ cups finely chopped walnuts, divided
½ cup apricot preserves

   Beat butter at medium speed of an electric mixer until creamy; gradually add sugar, beating well. Add egg yolk and lemon rind; beat well.
   Combine dry ingredients and 1 cup walnuts; stir into creamed mixture. Cover and chill at least 30 minutes.
   Shape dough into 1-inch balls. Beat egg white lightly. Dip balls in egg white; roll in remaining walnuts, and place on greased cookie sheets.
   Make an indentation in center of each cookie; fill with preserves. Bake at 350° for 20 minutes. Cool on wire racks. **Yield: 3 dozen.**

Gingersnaps

(pictured on page 2)

¾ cup shortening
1 cup sugar
1 large egg
¼ cup molasses
2 cups all-purpose flour
2 teaspoons baking soda
¼ teaspoon salt
½ teaspoon ground cinnamon
1 tablespoon ground ginger
Sugar

   Beat shortening at medium speed of an electric mixer until fluffy; gradually add 1 cup sugar, beating well. Add egg and molasses; mix well.
   Combine flour and next 4 ingredients; mix well. Add about one-fourth of flour mixture at a time to creamed mixture, beating until smooth after each addition. Cover and chill at least 1 hour.
   Shape dough into 1-inch balls; roll in sugar. Place on ungreased cookie sheets. Bake at 375° for 10 minutes. Cool on wire racks. **Yield: 4 dozen.**

Spice-Molasses Cookies

Spice-Molasses Cookies

¾ cup shortening
1 cup sugar
1 large egg
¼ cup molasses
2 cups all-purpose flour
1 teaspoon baking soda
1 teaspoon baking powder
¼ teaspoon salt
1 teaspoon ground ginger
1 teaspoon ground cinnamon
½ teaspoon ground nutmeg
¼ teaspoon ground cloves
¼ teaspoon ground allspice
Sugar

Beat shortening at medium speed of an electric mixer until fluffy; gradually add 1 cup sugar, beating well. Add egg and molasses; mix well.

Combine flour and next 8 ingredients; mix well. Add about one-fourth of flour mixture at a time to creamed mixture, beating until smooth after each addition. Cover and chill 1 hour.

Shape dough into 1-inch balls, and roll in sugar. Place 2 inches apart on ungreased cookie sheets. Bake at 375° for 9 to 11 minutes. (Tops will crack.) Cool on wire racks. **Yield: 4 dozen.**

Crispy Coconut-Oatmeal Cookies

Crispy Coconut-Oatmeal Cookies

1 cup shortening
1 cup sugar
1 cup firmly packed brown sugar
2 large eggs
1 teaspoon vanilla extract
2 cups all-purpose flour
1 teaspoon baking soda
½ teaspoon baking powder
½ teaspoon salt
2 cups regular oats, uncooked
2 cups crisp rice cereal
1 cup flaked coconut

Beat first 3 ingredients at medium speed of an electric mixer until blended; add eggs and vanilla, beating well.

Combine flour and next 3 ingredients; add to creamed mixture, mixing well. Stir in oats and remaining ingredients.

Shape dough into 1-inch balls, and place 2 inches apart on lightly greased cookie sheets; flatten slightly with a fork. Bake at 350° for 12 minutes or until done. Transfer to wire racks to cool. **Yield: 7 dozen.**

Special Oatmeal Cookies

1½ cups all-purpose flour
1 teaspoon baking soda
1 teaspoon salt
2 teaspoons ground cinnamon
½ teaspoon ground nutmeg
1 cup shortening
1 cup sugar
1 cup firmly packed brown sugar
2 large eggs
1 teaspoon lemon extract
3 cups quick-cooking oats, uncooked
1 cup chopped pecans

Combine first 5 ingredients; set aside.

Beat shortening at medium speed of an electric mixer until fluffy; add sugars, beating well. Add eggs and lemon extract, and beat well. Add flour mixture, mixing well. Stir in oats and pecans.

Shape dough into 1-inch balls, and place on lightly greased cookie sheets. Bake at 350° for 10 to 12 minutes. **Yield: 5 dozen.**

Old-Fashioned Peanut Butter Cookies

(pictured on cover and page 11)

1 cup butter or margarine, softened
1 cup creamy peanut butter
1 cup sugar
1 cup firmly packed brown sugar
2 large eggs, beaten
1 tablespoon milk
2½ cups all-purpose flour
2 teaspoons baking soda
¼ teaspoon salt
1 teaspoon vanilla extract
Additional sugar

Beat butter and peanut butter at medium speed of an electric mixer until creamy; gradually add 1 cup sugar and brown sugar, beating well. Add eggs and milk, beating well.

Combine flour, soda, and salt; add to creamed mixture, beating well. Stir in vanilla. Cover and chill 2 to 3 hours.

Shape dough into 1¼-inch balls; place 3 inches apart on ungreased cookie sheets. Dip a fork in sugar, and flatten cookies in a crisscross pattern. Bake at 375° for 10 minutes. Remove cookies to wire racks to cool. **Yield: 6 dozen.**

Double-Chip Peanut Butter Cookies

1 cup butter or margarine, softened
1 cup creamy peanut butter
2 cups firmly packed brown sugar
2 large eggs
1 teaspoon vanilla extract
1¼ cups all-purpose flour
1¼ cups whole wheat flour
1½ teaspoons baking soda
⅔ cup sesame seeds, toasted
½ teaspoon ground nutmeg
⅔ cup semisweet chocolate morsels
⅔ cup peanut butter morsels

Beat butter and peanut butter at medium speed of an electric mixer until creamy; gradually add brown sugar, beating well. Add eggs and vanilla, mixing well.

Combine all-purpose flour and next 4 ingredients; add to creamed mixture, and beat until smooth. Stir in morsels.

Shape dough into 1-inch balls. Place on lightly greased cookie sheets. Bake at 350° for 11 to 13 minutes. Cool on wire racks. **Yield: 7 dozen.**

Peanut Butter and Chocolate Chunk Cookies

½ cup butter or margarine, softened
¾ cup sugar
⅔ cup firmly packed brown sugar
2 egg whites
1¼ cups chunky peanut butter
1½ teaspoons vanilla extract
1 cup all-purpose flour
½ teaspoon baking soda
¼ teaspoon salt
5 (2.1-ounce) chocolate-covered crispy peanut-buttery candy bars, cut into ½-inch pieces

Beat butter at medium speed of an electric mixer until creamy; gradually add sugars, beating well. Add egg whites, beating well. Stir in peanut butter and vanilla.

Combine flour, soda, and salt; gradually add to creamed mixture, mixing well. Stir in candy.

Shape dough into 1½-inch balls, and place 2 inches apart on lightly greased cookie sheets.

Bake at 350° for 11 minutes or until browned. Cool 3 minutes on cookie sheets; transfer to wire racks to cool completely. **Yield: 4 dozen.**

Note: For chocolate-covered crispy peanut-buttery candy bars, we used Butterfingers.

Crisp Peanuttiest Cookies

½ cup butter or margarine, softened
½ cup chunky peanut butter
1½ cups firmly packed brown sugar
¾ cup sugar
2 large eggs
2½ cups all-purpose flour
1 teaspoon baking soda
½ cup flaked coconut
¾ cup Spanish peanuts

Beat butter and peanut butter at medium speed of an electric mixer until creamy; gradually add sugars, beating well. Add eggs, and mix well.

Combine flour and soda; add to creamed mixture, mixing well. Stir in coconut and peanuts.

Shape dough into 1-inch balls, and place on ungreased cookie sheets. Bake at 350° for 12 to 15 minutes or until lightly browned. Cool on wire racks. **Yield: 6 dozen.**

Crisp Peanuttiest Cookies

Chocolate-Ginger Crinkles

Chocolate-Ginger Crinkles

⅔ cup shortening
1 cup sugar
1 large egg
¼ cup molasses
2¼ cups all-purpose flour
1½ teaspoons baking soda
½ teaspoon salt
1 tablespoon ground ginger
2 (1-ounce) squares unsweetened chocolate, melted and cooled
Sugar

Beat shortening at medium speed of an electric mixer until fluffy; gradually add 1 cup sugar, beating well. Add egg, and beat well. Stir in molasses.

Combine flour and next 3 ingredients; add to creamed mixture, stirring well. Stir in melted chocolate.

Shape dough into 1-inch balls; roll balls in sugar. Place 2 inches apart on lightly greased cookie sheets. Bake at 350° for 10 to 12 minutes. Cool on wire racks. **Yield: 4 dozen.**

Double-Chocolate Sugar Cookies

1 (12-ounce) package semisweet chocolate morsels, divided
1 cup butter or margarine, softened
1 cup sugar
1 large egg
2 tablespoons milk
1 teaspoon vanilla extract
3 cups all-purpose flour
1 teaspoon baking powder
½ teaspoon baking soda
½ teaspoon salt
½ cup sugar

Melt 1 cup semisweet chocolate morsels in a heavy saucepan over low heat, reserving remaining morsels. Set aside.

Beat butter at medium speed of an electric mixer until creamy; gradually add 1 cup sugar, beating well. Add egg, milk, and vanilla, mixing well. Add melted morsels, mixing until blended.

Combine flour and next 3 ingredients; gradually add to creamed mixture, mixing well. Stir in remaining chocolate morsels.

Shape dough into balls, 1 tablespoon at a time; roll balls in ½ cup sugar. Place on lightly greased cookie sheets.

Bake at 400° for 8 to 10 minutes. (Cookies will be soft and will firm up as they cool.) Remove to wire racks to cool. **Yield: 4½ dozen.**

Cocoa Kiss Cookies

1 cup butter or margarine, softened
⅔ cup sugar
1 teaspoon vanilla extract
1⅔ cups all-purpose flour
¼ cup cocoa
1 cup coarsely ground walnuts
1 (9-ounce) package milk chocolate kisses, unwrapped

Beat butter at medium speed of an electric mixer until creamy; gradually add sugar, beating well. Add vanilla, mixing well. Add flour and cocoa, mixing well. Stir in walnuts. Cover and chill 2 hours or until firm.

Wrap 1 tablespoon of dough around each chocolate kiss, and roll to form a ball. Place on ungreased cookie sheets. Bake at 375° for 12 minutes. Cool slightly on cookie sheets; remove to wire racks. **Yield: about 4 dozen.**

Chocolate-Peanut Butter Snacks

22   Shapes of All Varieties

Chocolate-Peanut Butter Snacks

¾ cup creamy peanut butter
80 round buttery crackers
16 (1-ounce) squares chocolate-flavored candy
    coating
2 (1-ounce) squares vanilla-flavored candy
    coating
Orange paste food coloring

Spread 1 teaspoonful peanut butter on half of crackers; top with remaining crackers. Set aside.

Melt chocolate-flavored candy coating in a heavy saucepan over low heat; dip sandwich crackers in melted coating, allowing excess to drain. Place on wax paper to cool.

Melt vanilla-flavored candy coating in a heavy saucepan over low heat; add orange food coloring, stirring well. Place mixture in a heavy-duty zip-top plastic bag; seal. Using scissors, snip a tiny hole in corner of bag; drizzle candy-coating mixture in a zigzag pattern on top of crackers.
Yield: 40 snacks.

Chocolate-Tipped Butter Cookies

1 cup butter or margarine, softened
½ cup sifted powdered sugar
1 teaspoon vanilla extract
2 cups all-purpose flour
1 (6-ounce) package semisweet chocolate
    morsels
1 tablespoon shortening
½ cup finely chopped pecans

Beat butter at medium speed of an electric mixer until creamy; gradually add sugar, beating until light and fluffy. Stir in vanilla. Gradually add flour; mix well.

Shape dough into 2½- x ½-inch sticks. Place dough on ungreased cookie sheets. Flatten three-quarters of each cookie lengthwise with tines of a fork to ¼-inch thickness. Bake at 350° for 12 to 14 minutes. Remove to wire racks to cool.

Melt chocolate morsels and shortening in a heavy saucepan over low heat. Stir occasionally until thoroughly melted.

Dip unflattened tips of cookies in warm chocolate to coat both sides; roll tips in chopped pecans. Place cookies on wire racks until chocolate is firm.

Arrange cookies between layers of wax paper in an airtight container; store in a cool place.
Yield: 4 dozen.

Swedish Heirloom Cookies

½ cup shortening
½ cup butter or margarine, softened
1 cup sifted powdered sugar
½ teaspoon salt
2 cups all-purpose flour
1 tablespoon water
1 tablespoon vanilla extract
1¼ cups ground almonds
Powdered sugar

Beat shortening and butter at medium speed of an electric mixer until fluffy. Add 1 cup powdered sugar and salt; mix well. Stir in flour. Add water, vanilla, and almonds, stirring well.

Shape dough into 1-inch balls. Place on ungreased cookie sheets and flatten. Bake at 325° for 12 to 15 minutes or until done. Dredge warm cookies in powdered sugar. Yield: 4 dozen.

Sweet Ravioli

1 cup butter or margarine, softened
⅔ cup sugar
1 large egg, beaten
1 teaspoon grated lemon rind
1½ teaspoons vanilla extract
¼ teaspoon almond extract
2½ cups all-purpose flour
¼ teaspoon baking soda
⅛ teaspoon salt
About ½ cup raspberry preserves
Sifted powdered sugar

Beat butter at medium speed of an electric mixer until creamy; gradually add ⅔ cup sugar, beating well. Add egg, lemon rind, and extracts; mix well.

Combine flour, soda, and salt; add to creamed mixture. Divide dough in half. Roll each portion of dough between 2 sheets of wax paper to a 12-inch square. Cover and chill at least 1 hour.

Remove one portion of dough from refrigerator; remove top piece of wax paper, and cut dough into 1½-inch squares. Place ¼ teaspoon raspberry preserves in center of half of squares; brush edges of filled squares with water. Place unfilled squares over filled squares; press edges to seal. Cut an X on top of each. Repeat with remaining dough and preserves.

Place cookies on greased cookie sheets, and bake at 350° for 9 to 11 minutes or until edges are lightly browned. Remove from oven, and cool on cookie sheets 4 to 5 minutes. Transfer cookies to wire racks, and cool completely. Sprinkle with powdered sugar. **Yield: 64 cookies.**

Almond-Filled Wafers

1 cup butter or margarine, softened
2¼ cups all-purpose flour
⅓ cup whipping cream
½ cup sugar
¼ cup butter or margarine, softened
¾ cup sifted powdered sugar
½ teaspoon almond extract
1 or 2 drops of liquid food coloring (optional)

Beat 1 cup butter at medium speed of an electric mixer until butter is creamy. Gradually add flour alternately with whipping cream, beginning and ending with flour. Shape dough into a ball; cover and chill 2 hours.

Divide dough in half; store 1 portion of dough in refrigerator. Roll remaining portion to ⅛-inch thickness on a lightly floured surface. Cut with a 1½-inch round cookie cutter. Use a ¼- to ⅜-inch cutter to cut out heart or other decorative design in center of half of cookies.

Sprinkle both sides of cookies with sugar, and place on ungreased cookie sheets. Repeat procedure with remaining dough. Bake at 375° for 7 to 9 minutes or until very lightly browned. Cool on wire racks.

Combine ¼ cup butter, powdered sugar, and almond extract, mixing well. Add food coloring, if desired. Spread each solid cookie with a thin layer of filling. Top with decorative cookie. (Cookies are very delicate and must be handled carefully.) **Yield: about 4½ dozen.**

Cookie Tip

Carefully remove delicate cookies from a cookie sheet to a cooling rack. If they fall apart or crumble as you are transferring them with a spatula, wait a minute until they firm up before removing the remaining cookies from the cookie sheet.

Cherry Bonbon Cookies

Shape 1 rounded teaspoon dough around each chocolate piece, forming a 1-inch ball. Place on lightly greased cookie sheets.

Bake at 350° for 12 to 14 minutes or until lightly browned. Cool. Drizzle candy coating over cookies. **Yield: 4 dozen.**

Cherry Bonbon Cookies

24 maraschino cherries, undrained
½ cup butter or margarine, softened
¾ cup sifted powdered sugar
1½ cups all-purpose flour
⅛ teaspoon salt
2 tablespoons half-and-half
1 teaspoon vanilla extract
Powdered sugar
Cherry Glaze

Drain cherries, reserving ¼ cup juice for glaze; set aside.

Beat butter at medium speed of an electric mixer until creamy; gradually add ¾ cup sugar, beating well. Stir in flour and next 3 ingredients.

Shape dough into 24 balls. Press each ball around a cherry, covering completely; place on ungreased cookie sheets. Bake at 350° for 18 to 20 minutes. Remove to wire racks to cool completely. Sprinkle with powdered sugar, and drizzle with Cherry Glaze. **Yield: 2 dozen.**

Cherry Glaze
2 tablespoons butter or margarine, melted
1 cup sifted powdered sugar
¼ cup reserved cherry juice
Red food coloring (optional)

Combine first 3 ingredients; add food coloring, if desired. Place in a heavy-duty, zip-top plastic bag; seal. To drizzle, snip a tiny hole at one corner of bag and squeeze. **Yield: ½ cup.**

Surprise Bonbon Cookies

2 cups all-purpose flour
½ teaspoon salt
¾ cup butter or margarine, softened
½ cup sugar
2 egg yolks
1 (3.5-ounce) package almond paste or ⅓ cup almond paste
1 teaspoon vanilla extract
6 (1-ounce) squares semisweet chocolate or vanilla, each cut into 8 pieces
8 ounces chocolate-flavored candy coating, melted

Combine flour and salt in a small bowl; set mixture aside.

Beat butter at medium speed of an electric mixer until creamy; add sugar, beating well. Add egg yolks, almond paste, and vanilla; beat well. Add flour mixture, mixing well.

Devilish Marshmallow Cookies

½ cup shortening
1 cup sugar
2 large eggs
1¾ cups all-purpose flour
1 teaspoon baking soda
¼ teaspoon salt
½ cup cocoa
1 teaspoon vanilla extract
1 teaspoon butter flavoring
About 21 large marshmallows, cut in half
Frosting

Beat shortening at medium speed of an electric mixer until fluffy; gradually add sugar, beating well. Add eggs, one at a time, beating after each addition.

Combine flour, soda, salt, and cocoa; add to creamed mixture, mixing well. Stir in flavorings. (Dough will be stiff.) Cover and chill at least 30 minutes.

Shape dough into 1-inch balls; place on greased cookie sheets. Bake at 350° for 7 minutes. Place a marshmallow half on top of each cookie; bake 2 additional minutes. Cool on wire racks, and spread frosting over tops. **Yield: about 3½ dozen.**

Frosting

½ cup semisweet chocolate morsels
¼ cup milk
2 tablespoons butter or margarine
2 cups sifted powdered sugar
Milk (optional)

Combine first 3 ingredients in a saucepan. Cook over low heat, stirring constantly, until chocolate melts. Add powdered sugar, and beat until smooth. Add additional milk to frosting mixture, if needed, for proper spreading consistency. **Yield: 1 cup.**

Chocolate-Almond Balls

1 (9-ounce) package chocolate wafer cookies, crushed
1 cup finely chopped almonds, toasted
1 cup sifted powdered sugar
¼ cup light corn syrup
⅓ cup chocolate-flavored liqueur
1 pound vanilla-flavored candy coating
2 (1-ounce) squares semisweet chocolate

Combine first 5 ingredients in a large bowl; stir well. Shape into 1-inch balls; cover and chill until firm.

Melt candy coating in a heavy saucepan over low heat, stirring frequently. Dip chocolate balls in melted candy coating, and coat well. Place on wax paper to dry.

Melt chocolate in a small saucepan over low heat, stirring constantly. Remove from heat; stir well. Drizzle over candy-coated balls. Store in an airtight container. **Yield: about 4 dozen.**

Bourbon-Rum Balls

1 (12-ounce) package vanilla wafers
1 (16-ounce) package pecan pieces
½ cup honey
⅓ cup bourbon
⅓ cup dark rum
Sugar or vanilla wafer crumbs

Position knife blade in food processor bowl; add vanilla wafers. Process until fine. Transfer to a large bowl. Place pecans in processor bowl; process until finely chopped. Stir into vanilla wafer crumbs. Stir in honey, bourbon, and rum.

Shape mixture into 1-inch balls, and roll in sugar or additional vanilla wafer crumbs. Place in an airtight container, and store in refrigerator up to one month. **Yield: 6 dozen.**

Chocolate-Almond Balls

White Chocolate Truffles

White Chocolate Truffles

½ pound white chocolate, chopped
⅓ cup butter, softened and divided
⅓ cup sifted powdered sugar
2 tablespoons Frangelico liqueur
1 cup toasted, ground hazelnuts

Place white chocolate and 1 tablespoon butter in top of a double boiler; bring water to a boil. Reduce heat to low; cook until white chocolate melts. Remove from heat. Add remaining butter, powdered sugar, and liqueur; beat at low speed of an electric mixer until smooth. Cover and chill 1 hour or until firm.

Shape mixture into 1-inch balls, using a tiny ice cream scoop. Roll balls in ground hazelnuts. Place in miniature paper liners or foil cups. Cover and chill. Serve at room temperature. **Yield: 2 dozen.**

White Chocolate Truffles Technique

Hazelnuts have bitter brown skins that can be removed by baking at 350° for 15 minutes and rubbing briskly with a towel.

Mocha Surprise Truffles

1 (11.5-ounce) package milk chocolate morsels
½ cup sweetened condensed milk
2 tablespoons Kahlúa or other coffee-flavored liqueur
1 tablespoon plus 1 teaspoon instant coffee granules
⅛ teaspoon salt
26 chocolate-coated coffee beans
Chocolate sprinkles
Cocoa
Sifted powdered sugar

Place chocolate morsels in top of a double boiler. Bring water to a boil; reduce heat to low, and cook until chocolate melts. Stir in milk, Kahlúa, coffee granules, and salt. Cook until mixture is smooth. Remove from heat; cover and chill 30 minutes or until firm.

Shape 1 level tablespoon chocolate mixture around each coffee bean. Roll in chocolate sprinkles, cocoa, or powdered sugar. Place truffles in miniature paper liners. Store in refrigerator. **Yield: 26 truffles.**

Mocha Surprise Truffles Technique

Shape 1 tablespoon truffle mixture around a candy coffee bean. Roll truffles in chocolate sprinkles, cocoa, or powdered sugar.

From left: Spiced Shortbread Cookies, Cocoa Shortbread Wafers, Orange Shortbread Madeleines, Praline Shortbread Cookies, and Old-Fashioned Shortbread Cookie (lower right)

Cocoa Shortbread Wafers

1 cup butter, softened
¾ cup sifted powdered sugar
¼ cup cocoa
1½ cups all-purpose flour
Sugar

Beat butter at medium speed of an electric mixer until creamy; gradually add powdered sugar, beating well. Add cocoa, and beat mixture well. Stir in flour. (Dough will be stiff.)

Press dough into a lightly greased 15- x 10- x 1-inch jellyroll pan; prick all over with a fork. Bake at 300° for 30 minutes or until done. While warm, cut into 1½-inch diamonds, using a fluted pastry wheel, and sprinkle with sugar. Let cool in pan. **Yield: about 7½ dozen.**

Praline Shortbread Cookies

1 cup butter, softened
¾ cup firmly packed dark brown sugar
1½ cups all-purpose flour
½ cup ground pecans

Beat butter at medium speed of an electric mixer until creamy; gradually add brown sugar, beating well. Stir in flour and ground pecans. (Dough will be stiff.)

Divide dough into 6 equal portions; pat each portion into a 6-inch circle on lightly greased cookie sheets. Score dough into 8 wedges, using a fluted pastry wheel. Press outside edges of dough with tines of a fork.

Bake at 325° for 20 minutes or until cookies are lightly browned. Let cool on cookie sheets; break into wedges. **Yield: 4 dozen.**

Spiced Shortbread Cookies

1 cup butter or margarine, softened
⅔ cup sifted powdered sugar
½ teaspoon ground nutmeg
½ teaspoon ground cinnamon
½ teaspoon ground ginger
2 cups all-purpose flour

Beat butter at medium speed of an electric mixer until creamy; gradually add sugar, beating well. Add spices, and beat well. Stir in flour. (Dough will be stiff.)

Shape dough into 1¼-inch balls, and place 2 inches apart on lightly greased cookie sheets. Lightly press cookies with a floured cookie stamp or fork to flatten to ¼-inch thickness.

Bake at 325° for 15 to 18 minutes or until done. Let cool on wire racks. **Yield: 2½ dozen.**

Old-Fashioned Shortbread Cookie

1 cup butter, softened
¾ cup sifted powdered sugar
¼ cup cornstarch
1¾ cups all-purpose flour

Beat butter at medium speed of an electric mixer until creamy; gradually add powdered sugar and cornstarch, beating well. Stir in flour. (Dough will be stiff.)

Press dough into a lightly greased and floured 9-inch cookie mold or cakepan. Bake at 325° for 30 to 35 minutes or until done. Invert cookie from pan, and let cool on wire rack. Yield: **1 (9-inch) cookie.**

Note: May be baked in 5-inch cookie molds. Firmly press about ¼ cup dough into lightly greased and floured molds, and invert onto lightly greased cookie sheets. Bake at 325° for 15 to 20 minutes or until done. **Yield: about 10 cookies.**

Orange Shortbread Madeleines

1 cup butter, softened
¾ cup sifted powdered sugar
1 teaspoon grated orange rind
1 teaspoon orange extract
1¾ cups all-purpose flour
Vegetable cooking spray

Beat butter at medium speed of an electric mixer until creamy; gradually add sugar, beating well. Add orange rind and extract. Stir in flour. (Dough will be stiff.)

Press about 1½ tablespoons dough into madeleine molds lightly sprayed with cooking spray. Bake at 325° for 20 minutes or until done. Invert onto wire racks to cool. **Yield: 2½ dozen.**

Delicate Madeleines

Delicate Madeleines

1 large egg
⅛ teaspoon salt
3 tablespoons sugar
¼ cup all-purpose flour
½ teaspoon grated orange rind
¼ cup butter, melted and cooled
Powdered sugar

Beat egg and salt at high speed of an electric mixer until foamy. Gradually add 3 tablespoons sugar; beat at high speed 10 to 15 minutes or until mixture is thickened.

Combine flour and orange rind; gradually fold into egg mixture, 2 tablespoons at a time. Gradually fold in melted butter, 1 tablespoon at a time.

Spoon batter into greased and floured 3-inch madeleine molds. Bake at 400° for 8 to 10 minutes or until lightly browned. Let cool in molds 3 minutes. Remove from molds, and let cool on a wire rack, flat side down. Dust lightly with powdered sugar. **Yield: 1 dozen.**

Delicate Madeleines Technique

Spoon batter into a greased and floured madeleine mold, a special pan with a scallop-shell design.

Spritz Hearts

2 cups butter, softened
1 cup sugar
4 egg yolks
4 cups all-purpose flour
1 to 2 teaspoons vanilla extract
3 or 4 drops of red liquid food coloring
24 ounces vanilla-flavored candy coating

Beat butter at medium speed of an electric mixer; gradually add sugar, beating well. Add egg yolks, mixing well. Add flour; stir in vanilla and food coloring.

Use a cookie gun, following manufacturer's instructions, to shape cookies into hearts or other shapes as desired. Place cookies on ungreased cookie sheets.

Bake at 375° for 8 to 10 minutes or until cookies are lightly browned. Let cool completely on wire racks.

Melt candy coating in a large heavy saucepan over low heat. Dip half of each heart into coating; place on wax paper to cool. Store in airtight containers, placing wax paper between each layer. **Yield: 12 dozen.**

Did You Know?

Madeleines are spongecake-like cookies baked in a special pan with scallop-shell indentations. When baked and removed from the pan, madeleines take the form of the shell.

Spritz are rich, buttery cookies that are shaped by forcing the dough through a cookie gun or press. The name comes from *spritzen*, which is German for "to squirt or spray."

Almond Spritz Cookies

1 cup butter, softened
⅔ cup sugar
3 egg yolks
1 teaspoon vanilla extract
2½ cups all-purpose flour
⅛ teaspoon salt
1 egg white, lightly beaten
½ cup ground blanched almonds
1 (12-ounce) package semisweet chocolate
 morsels

Beat butter at medium speed of an electric mixer until creamy; gradually add sugar, beating well. Add egg yolks, one at a time, beating well. Stir in vanilla. Combine flour and salt; add to creamed mixture, beating well.

Use a cookie press, following manufacturer's instructions, to shape dough into 2½-inch-long cookies, or use the following procedure: Sift powdered sugar lightly over work surface. Shape 3 tablespoons dough by hand into a 2½-inch-long rope; repeat with remaining dough. Place on lightly greased cookie sheets.

Brush each cookie with egg white, and lightly sprinkle with almonds (reserve remaining almonds). Bake at 400° for 8 to 10 minutes or until lightly browned. (Cookies rolled by hand may require 2 to 3 minutes additional baking.) Remove cookies to wire racks; cool completely.

Melt chocolate morsels in a heavy saucepan over low heat; remove from heat. Dip ends of cookies in chocolate, covering about ½ inch on each end. Sprinkle ends with remaining almonds. Place cookies on wire racks until chocolate is firm. **Yield: about 6 dozen.**

Melt-Away Butter Cookies

(pictured on page 2)

1¼ cups butter, softened
¾ cup sifted powdered sugar
2½ cups all-purpose flour
½ teaspoon vanilla extract
½ teaspoon almond extract
Few drops of liquid food coloring (optional)

Beat butter at medium speed of electric mixer until creamy; gradually add sugar, beating well. Add flour, and mix well. Stir in flavorings and food coloring, if desired.

Use a cookie gun to shape dough as desired, following the manufacturer's instructions. Place cookies on ungreased cookie sheets.

Bake at 325° for 15 minutes. Cool on wire racks. Store in airtight containers, placing wax paper between each layer. **Yield: about 7 dozen (2-inch) cookies.**

Variation

Chocolate-Tipped Butter Cookies: Melt 1 (12-ounce) package semisweet chocolate morsels and 1 tablespoon shortening in a heavy saucepan over low heat. Dip half of each prepared butter cookie in chocolate mixture. Roll chocolate-dipped portion in ½ cup finely chopped pecans. Place cookies on wire racks until chocolate is firm.

Cookie Tip

Use a cookie gun to stamp out a wide variety of perfectly shaped cookies in a minimum of time. Electric and hand-pump models of cookie guns are available in most kitchen shops or department stores. Most are constructed to also make mints, cheese straws, or canapés. Be sure to follow manufacturer's directions.

Butter Cookies

1 cup butter or margarine, softened
¾ cup sugar
1 large egg
½ teaspoon vanilla extract
2½ cups all-purpose flour
1 teaspoon baking powder
¼ teaspoon salt
Food coloring (optional)
Buttercream Frosting
Assorted candies and sprinkles

Beat butter at medium speed of an electric mixer until creamy; gradually add sugar, beating well. Add egg and vanilla; beat well.

Combine flour, baking powder, and salt; add to creamed mixture, mixing well. Color dough with food coloring, if desired. Use a cookie press to shape dough as desired. Place cookies on ungreased cookie sheets.

Bake at 350° for 10 to 12 minutes. Cool on wire racks. Decorate with Buttercream Frosting, assorted candies, and decorator sprinkles. **Yield: about 6 dozen (2-inch) cookies.**

Buttercream Frosting

3 tablespoons butter or margarine, softened
2⅓ cups sifted powdered sugar
Dash of salt
1½ to 2 tablespoons milk
½ teaspoon vanilla extract
Food coloring (optional)

Beat butter at medium speed of an electric mixer until creamy; gradually add powdered sugar, beating well. Add salt, milk, and vanilla; mix well. Color frosting with food coloring, if desired. **Yield: about 1 cup.**

Turkey Treats

1 (16-ounce) package cream-filled chocolate sandwich cookies
¼ cup red cinnamon candies
1¼ cups malted milk balls
1 (16-ounce) container ready-to-spread chocolate frosting
1 (9½-ounce) package candy corn

Separate each cookie, leaving cream filling on one side; set aside halves without filling.

To make a turkey body, attach or "glue" a cinnamon candy (for turkey head) to each malted milk ball (turkey body) with a dab of chocolate frosting. Attach a turkey body to center of each cookie half with cream filling, using a dab of chocolate frosting.

Spread chocolate frosting on the inside of each cookie half that does not have cream filling. For the turkey tail, arrange candy corn on chocolate-frosting cookies with wide end of candy along outer edge.

Attach each turkey tail behind a turkey body, using chocolate frosting. Store assembled turkeys in the refrigerator. **Yield: 42 cookies.**

Turkey Treats Technique

While you're preparing the big Thanksgiving feast, keep the kids busy making their own tasty turkeys.

Jack-O'-Lantern Cookies

½ cup butter or margarine, softened
1 cup sugar
1 cup canned or mashed cooked pumpkin
1 tablespoon grated orange rind
2 cups all-purpose flour
1 teaspoon baking powder
1 teaspoon baking soda
¼ teaspoon salt
1 teaspoon ground cinnamon
½ cup raisins
½ cup chopped pecans
Frosting
Decorative candies (optional)

Combine first 4 ingredients in a large bowl; beat at medium speed of an electric mixer until blended.

Combine flour and next 4 ingredients; beat at low speed of an electric mixer until blended. Stir in raisins and pecans.

Drop cookie dough by heaping tablespoonfuls 4 inches apart onto lightly greased cookie sheets. Lightly press each cookie into a 3½-inch circle with fingertips dipped in flour.

Bake at 375° for 16 to 18 minutes or until brown. Cool cookies completely on wire racks. Spread frosting on tops of cookies. Decorate with raisins, candy corn, chocolate morsels, and cinnamon candies, if desired. **Yield: 1½ dozen cookies.**

Frosting

3 tablespoons butter or margarine, softened
3 cups sifted powdered sugar
3 to 4 tablespoons milk
1½ teaspoons vanilla extract
3 drops of red liquid food coloring
3 drops of yellow liquid food coloring

Combine butter, powdered sugar, and 3 tablespoons milk in a small bowl; beat at high speed of an electric mixer, gradually adding more milk, if necessary, to make a spreading consistency. Add vanilla and food colorings; beat until well mixed. **Yield: frosting for 1½ dozen cookies.**

Peppy Pumpkin Cookies

1 cup butter or margarine, softened
1¼ cups sifted powdered sugar
1 large egg
1½ teaspoons vanilla extract
½ teaspoon almond extract
2½ cups all-purpose flour
½ teaspoon salt
Green and orange paste food coloring
Pecan pieces
Chocolate morsels

Beat butter at medium speed of an electric mixer until creamy; gradually add powdered sugar, beating well. Add egg and extracts, beating until blended.

Combine flour and salt; add flour mixture to creamed mixture, mixing well.

Color ⅔ cup cookie dough with green food coloring. Color remaining dough with orange food coloring.

Spoon orange dough into a pastry bag fitted with metal tip No. 2110. Pipe mixture into pumpkin shapes on ungreased cookie sheets. Spoon green mixture into a pastry bag fitted with metal tip No. 10. Pipe green stems on each pumpkin.

Bake at 400° for 6 to 8 minutes. Immediately arrange pecan pieces and chocolate morsels to make pumpkin faces. Remove to wire racks to cool completely. **Yield: 3 dozen.**

Peppy Pumpkin Cookies

Snappin' Turtle Cookies

½ cup butter or margarine, softened
½ cup firmly packed brown sugar
1 large egg
1 large egg, separated
1 teaspoon vanilla extract
1½ cups all-purpose flour
¼ teaspoon baking soda
¼ teaspoon salt
12½ dozen pecan halves
Frosting

Beat butter at medium speed of an electric mixer until creamy; gradually add brown sugar, beating well. Add 1 egg, 1 egg yolk, and vanilla, beating until well blended.

Combine flour, soda, and salt; add to creamed mixture, mixing well. Cover and chill at least 1 hour. Arrange pecan halves in groups of 5 on ungreased cookie sheets, resembling head and legs of turtles.

Shape dough into 1-inch balls, and dip bottoms in remaining egg white. Press gently onto pecans to resemble turtle bodies.

Bake at 350° for 10 to 12 minutes. Cool on wire racks. Spread frosting on tops of cookies. **Yield: 2½ dozen.**

Frosting

2 (1-ounce) squares unsweetened chocolate
¼ cup milk
1 tablespoon butter or margarine
About 1¾ cups sifted powdered sugar

Combine chocolate, milk, and butter in a medium saucepan; cook over low heat, stirring constantly, until chocolate melts. Remove from heat. Add powdered sugar; beat until smooth. **Yield: about 1 cup.**

Chocolate Waffle Cookies

⅓ cup shortening
1 (1-ounce) square unsweetened chocolate
1 large egg, beaten
½ cup sugar
2 tablespoons milk
½ teaspoon vanilla extract
¾ cup all-purpose flour
½ teaspoon baking powder
¼ teaspoon salt
1 cup chopped pecans

Melt shortening and chocolate in a saucepan over low heat, stirring constantly; let cool.

Combine egg, sugar, milk, and vanilla in a mixing bowl; stir well. Add chocolate mixture; stir well. Combine flour, baking powder, and salt; add to chocolate mixture, stirring well. Stir in pecans.

Preheat waffle iron at medium heat. Drop dough by level tablespoonfuls 2 inches apart onto iron. Close iron; bake 3 to 4 minutes or until done. Remove to wire racks, and let cool completely. **Yield: 2 dozen.**

Chocolate Waffle Cookies Technique

Drop dough by level tablespoonfuls onto a preheated waffle iron. Close iron; bake cookies 3 to 4 minutes or until done.

Chocolate Waffle Cookies

Buttery Lace Cookies

Buttery Lace Cookies

½ cup firmly packed brown sugar
⅓ cup butter
2 tablespoons whipping cream
¾ cup minced almonds, pecans, or unsalted
    peanuts
3 tablespoons all-purpose flour

Combine first 3 ingredients in a saucepan. Bring to a boil over medium heat, stirring constantly. Remove from heat; stir in nuts and flour.

Spoon batter by tablespoonfuls 3 inches apart onto aluminum foil-lined or parchment paper-lined cookie sheets. Spread batter into circles, making 3 cookies at a time.

Bake at 350° for 6 to 8 minutes or until edges are lightly browned. (Cookies will spread during baking.) Remove from oven, and let cool slightly (about 1 minute).

Lift cookies with a metal spatula when cookies are cool enough to hold their shape. Flip cookies over, and roll each around the handle of a wooden spoon or other cylindrical object. Cool completely on wire racks. Remove wooden spoons when cookies have cooled. Continue procedure with remaining cookie batter. Store cooled cookies in an airtight container up to 1 week.
Yield: 1½ dozen.

Note: If baked cookies become too crisp to roll, reheat for 30 seconds.

Variation

Fill cooled cookies with whipped cream, or dip ends of cookies in 1 cup melted semisweet chocolate morsels, and let harden on wax paper.

Buttery Lace Cookies Techniques

Spoon cookie batter by tablespoonfuls onto a lined cookie sheet. Cookies will spread as they bake.

Let baked cookies cool slightly; then quickly roll each cookie around the handle of a wooden spoon.

For a special touch, pipe whipped cream into ends of cookies, or dip ends of cookies in melted chocolate.

French Curled Cookies

¼ cup plus 2 tablespoons butter or
    margarine, softened
1 cup sifted powdered sugar
⅔ cup all-purpose flour
4 egg whites
1 teaspoon vanilla extract

Beat butter at medium speed of an electric mixer until creamy; add sugar, beating well. Add flour, egg whites, and vanilla; mix well.

Divide a well-greased cookie sheet into four sections. Spoon 1½ teaspoons batter in center of each section. Spread each portion of batter evenly with a spatula to make a 4- x 3-inch oval. Bake at 425° for 3 minutes or until edges are golden.

Loosen cookies with a metal spatula, but leave on cookie sheet. Place one cookie upside down on counter, and quickly roll it lengthwise around the handle of a wooden spoon. Remove cookie, and let cool on wire rack.

Repeat procedure with remaining cookies as quickly as possible. (If cookies become too stiff before rolling, return cookie sheet to oven briefly to soften them.) Continue procedure with remaining cookie batter. **Yield: 3 dozen.**

Pizzelles

3 large eggs
¾ cup sugar
¾ cup butter or margarine, softened
1 teaspoon vanilla extract
¼ teaspoon anise oil
1½ cups all-purpose flour
1 teaspoon baking powder
Vegetable oil

Beat eggs at medium speed of an electric mixer until foamy; gradually add sugar, beating until thick and lemon colored. Add butter, vanilla, and anise oil; mix well. Add flour and baking powder; beat until smooth.

Brush pizzelle iron lightly with oil; preheat iron over medium heat 2 minutes. Place 1 tablespoon batter in center of iron; close iron, and bake 30 seconds on each side or until pizzelle is lightly browned. Repeat with remaining batter; cool on wire racks. **Yield: 2½ dozen.**

Rosettes

1 cup plus 1 tablespoon all-purpose flour
¼ teaspoon salt
1 cup milk
1 large egg
1 tablespoon sugar
1 tablespoon vanilla extract
Vegetable oil
Powdered sugar

Combine first 6 ingredients in a medium mixing bowl; beat at low speed of an electric mixer until blended and smooth. Cover and chill at least 30 minutes.

Pour oil to depth of 2 inches in a large skillet; heat oil to 370°. Heat rosette iron in hot oil about 1 minute. Drain excess oil from iron, and dip iron into batter, being careful not to coat top of iron with batter.

Dip iron into hot oil. As soon as rosette is formed (about 5 seconds), lift iron slowly up and down to release rosette from iron. (If necessary, push rosette gently with a fork to release.) Fry until golden, turning to brown other side. Drain upside-down on paper towels.

Reheat iron in oil for a few seconds, and repeat procedure for each shell. Dust lightly with powdered sugar. **Yield: 1 dozen (3-inch) rosettes.**

Drop and Bake

Nothing could be easier than drop cookies—simply mix and drop the dough by spoonfuls onto cookie sheets. Although chocolate chip ranks as the favorite, this collection offers tasty surprises in every bite.

Best-Ever Chocolate Chip Cookies, Super Chocolate Chunk Cookies

Carrot Cookies, Apple-Oatmeal Cookies, Cashew Crunch Cookies, Raisin Cookies

Orange-Chocolate Chip Cookies, Triple Chip Cookies, Loaded-with-Chips Cookies

Salted Peanut Cookies, Walnut Spice Kisses, Monster Cookies

Toasted Oat-Coconut Cookies (page 57)

Best-Ever Chocolate Chip Cookies

¾ cup butter or margarine, softened
¼ cup shortening
¾ cup sugar
¾ cup firmly packed brown sugar
2 large eggs
1 teaspoon vanilla extract
2¼ cups all-purpose flour
1 teaspoon baking soda
¼ teaspoon salt
1 (12-ounce) package semisweet chocolate
    morsels

Beat butter and shortening at medium speed of an electric mixer until fluffy; gradually add sugars, beating well. Add eggs and vanilla, beating well.

Combine flour, soda, and salt; add to creamed mixture, mixing well. Stir in chocolate morsels.

Drop dough by heaping teaspoonfuls onto ungreased cookie sheets. Bake at 375° for 9 to 11 minutes. Cool slightly on cookie sheets; remove to wire racks to cool completely. **Yield: about 6½ dozen.**

Variations

Double Chip Cookies: Prepare Best-Ever Chocolate Chip Cookies, using 1 cup peanut butter morsels or butterscotch morsels and 1 (6-ounce) package semisweet chocolate morsels instead of 1 (12-ounce) package semisweet chocolate morsels.

Jumbo Chocolate Chip Cookies: Prepare Best-Ever Chocolate Chip Cookies, dropping them onto ungreased cookie sheets by ¼ cupfuls. Lightly press each cookie into a 3-inch circle with fingertips. Bake at 350° for 15 to 17 minutes. **Yield: 1½ dozen.**

Loaded-with-Chips Cookies

(pictured on cover)

½ cup butter or margarine, softened
½ cup shortening
1 cup firmly packed brown sugar
½ cup sugar
2 large eggs
1 teaspoon vanilla extract
1½ cups regular oats, uncooked
1¾ cups all-purpose flour
1 teaspoon baking soda
½ teaspoon salt
1 (12-ounce) package semisweet chocolate
    morsels
¾ cup chopped pecans

Beat butter and shortening at medium speed of an electric mixer until fluffy; gradually add sugars, beating well. Add eggs and vanilla, beating well.

Combine oats, flour, soda, and salt; add to creamed mixture, mixing well. Stir in chocolate morsels and pecans.

Drop dough by heaping teaspoonfuls onto ungreased cookie sheets. Bake at 350° for 12 to 14 minutes or until lightly browned. Remove to wire racks to cool. **Yield: 6 dozen.**

Did You Know?

Ruth Wakefield, owner of the Toll House Inn near Boston, created the chocolate chip cookie in the 1930s. While making a batch of her favorite butter cookies, she chopped up some chocolate and added the pieces to the dough, expecting them to melt. Instead they softened slightly but kept their shape. She shared her surprise with a food company, and a new product was born.

Super Chocolate Chunk Cookies

1 cup butter or margarine, softened
1 cup sugar
½ cup firmly packed brown sugar
2 large eggs
2 teaspoons vanilla extract
2 cups all-purpose flour
1 teaspoon baking powder
½ teaspoon salt
1 (12-ounce) package semisweet chocolate
   chunks
1 cup chopped walnuts

Beat butter at medium speed of an electric mixer until creamy; gradually add sugars, beating well. Add eggs and vanilla, beating well.

Combine flour, baking powder, and salt; add to creamed mixture, mixing well. Stir in chocolate chunks and walnuts. Cover and chill at least 1 hour.

Drop dough by tablespoonfuls onto ungreased cookie sheets. Bake at 350° for 12 to 15 minutes or until lightly browned. Cool slightly on cookie sheets; transfer to wire racks to cool completely. **Yield: 4 dozen.**

Super Chocolate Chunk Cookies

Triple Chip Cookies

1 cup butter or margarine, softened
1 cup sugar
½ cup firmly packed brown sugar
2 large eggs
1 teaspoon vanilla extract
2¼ cups all-purpose flour
1 teaspoon baking soda
½ teaspoon salt
¾ cup semisweet chocolate morsels
¾ cup milk chocolate morsels
¾ cup vanilla milk morsels
½ cup chopped blanched almonds

Beat butter at medium speed of an electric mixer until creamy; gradually add sugars, beating well. Add eggs and vanilla; beat well.

Combine flour, soda, and salt; gradually add to creamed mixture, mixing well after each addition. Stir in morsels and almonds.

Drop dough by tablespoonfuls onto ungreased cookie sheets. Bake at 350° for 12 to 14 minutes or until lightly browned. Transfer cookies to wire racks, and let cool completely. **Yield: 4 dozen.**

Did You Know?

Despite its name and texture, white chocolate is actually not chocolate at all. It's a mixture of cocoa butter, milk solids, sugar, and vanilla; it lacks the cocoa solids that give dark chocolate its color and some of its flavor.

However, don't confuse white chocolate with vanilla-flavored candy coating. While the texture and look are much the same and the ingredients are similar, the cocoa butter is replaced with vegetable fat in candy coating.

Triple Chip Cookies Techniques

Stir semisweet chocolate morsels, milk chocolate morsels, and vanilla milk morsels into cookie batter.

Chop whole blanched almonds on a cutting board with a large chef's knife, often referred to as a French knife.

Drop cookie dough by tablespoonfuls onto ungreased cookie sheets; bake until cookies are lightly browned.

Triple Chip Cookies

Chocolate Oatmeal Chippers

Chocolate Oatmeal Chippers

1 cup butter or margarine, softened
1½ cups sugar
1 large egg
¼ cup water
1 teaspoon vanilla extract
1½ cups all-purpose flour
½ teaspoon baking soda
½ teaspoon salt
½ teaspoon ground cinnamon
½ teaspoon ground nutmeg
3 cups quick-cooking oats, uncooked
1 (6-ounce) package semisweet chocolate morsels
1 cup chopped pecans (optional)

Beat butter at medium speed of an electric mixer until creamy; gradually add sugar, beating well. Add egg, water, and vanilla, mixing well.

Combine flour, soda, salt, cinnamon, and nutmeg; add to creamed mixture, mixing well. Stir in oats, morsels, and pecans, if desired.

Drop dough by rounded teaspoonfuls onto ungreased cookie sheets. Bake at 350° for 10 to 12 minutes or until lightly browned. Cool slightly on cookie sheets; remove to wire racks to cool completely. **Yield: about 8 dozen.**

Variations

Raisin Oatmeal Cookies: Prepare Chocolate Oatmeal Chippers, deleting 1 (6-ounce) package semisweet chocolate morsels and adding 1 cup raisins.

Peanut Butter Oatmeal Chippers: Prepare Chocolate Oatmeal Chippers, using 1 cup peanut butter morsels instead of 1 (6-ounce) package semisweet chocolate morsels.

Chocolate Chippers

1 cup butter or margarine, softened
1 (8-ounce) package cream cheese, softened
1 cup sugar
1 cup firmly packed brown sugar
2 large eggs
1½ teaspoons vanilla extract
2 cups all-purpose flour
1½ cups quick-cooking oats, uncooked
1 teaspoon baking powder
1 teaspoon baking soda
½ teaspoon salt
1 cup (6 ounces) semisweet chocolate mini-morsels
1 cup (6 ounces) milk chocolate morsels or rainbow semisweet chocolate morsels
1½ cups chopped walnuts

Beat butter and cream cheese at medium speed of an electric mixer until fluffy; gradually add sugars, beating well. Add eggs and vanilla, mixing well.

Combine flour and next 4 ingredients; gradually add to creamed mixture, mixing well. Stir in chocolate morsels and walnuts.

Drop dough by rounded teaspoonfuls onto lightly greased cookie sheets. Bake at 350° for 12 to 14 minutes. Remove to wire racks to cool. **Yield: 8 dozen.**

Cookie Tip

Chocolate morsels can be stored up to 9 months. When conditions are too humid and warm, chocolate develops "bloom"—the morsels look gray on the surface. This doesn't affect quality and disappears when the chocolate is heated.

Measuring Morsels:
1 (6-ounce) package = 1 cup
1 (12-ounce) package = 2 cups

Brownie Chip Cookies

1 (23.7-ounce) package brownie mix
2 large eggs
⅓ cup vegetable oil
1 (6-ounce) package semisweet chocolate
    morsels
½ cup chopped pecans

Combine first 3 ingredients; beat about 50 strokes with a spoon. Stir in chocolate morsels and pecans.

Drop dough by rounded teaspoonfuls onto greased cookie sheets. Bake at 350° for 10 to 12 minutes. Cool slightly (about 2 minutes) on cookie sheets. Remove to wire racks, and let cool completely. **Yield: about 6 dozen.**

Monster Cookies

½ cup butter or margarine, softened
1 cup sugar
1 cup plus 2 tablespoons firmly packed brown
    sugar
3 large eggs
2 cups creamy peanut butter
¾ teaspoon light corn syrup
¼ teaspoon vanilla extract
4½ cups regular oats, uncooked
2 teaspoons baking soda
¼ teaspoon salt
1 cup candy-coated milk chocolate pieces
1 (6-ounce) package semisweet chocolate
    morsels

Beat butter at medium speed of an electric mixer until creamy; gradually add sugars, and beat well. Add eggs and next 3 ingredients; beat well. Add oats, soda, and salt; stir well. Stir in chocolate pieces and morsels. (Dough will be stiff.)

Pack dough into a ¼-cup measure. Drop dough

4 inches apart onto lightly greased cookie sheets. Lightly press each cookie into a 3½-inch circle with fingertips.

Bake at 350° for 12 to 15 minutes (centers of cookies will be slightly soft). Cool slightly on cookie sheets; remove to wire racks, and cool completely. **Yield: 2½ dozen.**

Backpack Cookies

1 cup butter or margarine, softened
1 cup sugar
1 cup firmly packed brown sugar
2 large eggs
1 teaspoon vanilla extract
2 cups all-purpose flour
½ teaspoon baking powder
1 teaspoon baking soda
⅛ teaspoon salt
2 cups regular oats, uncooked
2 cups oven-toasted rice cereal
1 cup candy-coated milk chocolate pieces
1 (6-ounce) package semisweet chocolate
    morsels
½ cup chopped unsalted roasted peanuts
½ cup chopped pecans
½ cup flaked coconut

Beat butter at medium speed of an electric mixer until creamy; gradually add sugars, beating well. Add eggs and vanilla; beat well.

Combine flour, baking powder, soda, and salt; add to creamed mixture, mixing well. Fold in oats and remaining ingredients.

Drop dough by rounded tablespoonfuls 2 inches apart onto ungreased cookie sheets. Bake at 350° for 10 to 12 minutes or until cookies are lightly browned. Transfer cookies to wire racks, and let cool completely. **Yield: 7½ dozen.**

Backpack Cookies

Orange-Chocolate Chip Cookies

½ cup shortening
1 (3-ounce) package cream cheese, softened
½ cup sugar
1 large egg
1 teaspoon vanilla extract
1 teaspoon grated orange rind
1 cup all-purpose flour
½ teaspoon salt
1 (6-ounce) package semisweet chocolate
   morsels

Combine first 4 ingredients in a large bowl; beat until smooth and creamy. Add vanilla and orange rind; beat well.

Combine flour and salt; add to creamed mixture, beating well. Stir in semisweet chocolate morsels.

Drop dough by heaping teaspoonfuls onto ungreased cookie sheets. Bake at 350° for 15 minutes or until edges just begin to brown. Cool on wire racks. **Yield: 3 dozen.**

Oatmeal-Peanut Butter-Chocolate Chip Cookies

½ cup butter or margarine, softened
1 (18-ounce) jar chunky peanut butter
1½ cups sugar
1½ cups firmly packed brown sugar
4 large eggs
1 teaspoon vanilla extract
6 cups quick-cooking oats, uncooked
2½ teaspoons baking soda
1 (6-ounce) package semisweet chocolate
   morsels

Beat butter and peanut butter at medium speed of an electric mixer until fluffy; gradually add sugars, beating well. Add eggs and vanilla, mixing well.

Combine oats and baking soda; add to creamed mixture, mixing well. Stir in morsels.

Drop dough by tablespoonfuls onto ungreased cookie sheets. Bake at 350° for 9 to 10 minutes. Cool on cookie sheets 5 minutes; remove to wire racks to cool completely. **Yield: 7 dozen.**

White Chocolate Chunk Cookies

½ cup butter or margarine, softened
½ cup shortening
¾ cup sugar
½ cup firmly packed brown sugar
1 large egg
2 cups all-purpose flour
1 teaspoon baking soda
½ teaspoon salt
2 teaspoons vanilla extract
10 ounces white chocolate, coarsely chopped
½ cup coarsely chopped macadamia nuts,
   lightly toasted

Beat butter and shortening at medium speed of an electric mixer until creamy; gradually add sugars, beating well. Add egg; beat well.

Combine flour, soda, and salt; add to creamed mixture, mixing well. Stir in vanilla. Stir in white chocolate and macadamia nuts. Cover and chill 1 hour.

Drop dough by 2 tablespoonfuls, 3 inches apart, onto lightly greased cookie sheets. Bake at 350° for 12 to 14 minutes (cookies will be soft). Cool slightly on cookie sheets; remove to wire racks to cool completely. **Yield: 1½ dozen.**

White Chocolate Chunk Cookies

Chunky Macadamia Nut-White Chocolate Cookies

½ cup butter or margarine, softened
¾ cup firmly packed brown sugar
2 tablespoons sugar
1 large egg
1½ teaspoons vanilla extract
2 cups all-purpose flour
¾ teaspoon baking soda
½ teaspoon baking powder
⅛ teaspoon salt
1 (6-ounce) package white chocolate-flavored baking bars, cut into chunks
1 (7-ounce) jar macadamia nuts, coarsely chopped

Beat butter at medium speed of an electric mixer until creamy; gradually add sugars, beating well. Add egg and vanilla, mixing well.

Combine flour and next 3 ingredients; gradually add to creamed mixture, mixing well. Stir in white chocolate chunks and nuts.

Drop by rounded teaspoonfuls onto lightly greased cookie sheets. Bake at 350° for 8 to 10 minutes or until lightly browned. Remove to wire racks to cool. **Yield: 5 dozen.**

Forget 'em Cookies

2 egg whites
½ teaspoon vanilla extract
¼ teaspoon cream of tartar
½ cup sugar
1 (6-ounce) package semisweet chocolate morsels
1 cup chopped pecans

Preheat oven to 350°. Beat egg whites, vanilla, and cream of tartar at high speed of an electric mixer until foamy. Gradually add sugar, 1 tablespoon at a time, beating until stiff peaks form and sugar dissolves (2 to 4 minutes). Fold in chocolate morsels and pecans.

Drop mixture by heaping teaspoonfuls onto cookie sheets lined with aluminum foil. Place in oven, and turn off heat immediately. Do not open oven door for at least 8 hours.

Remove cookies from foil. Store cookies in an airtight container up to 1 week. **Yield: 4½ dozen.**

Chocolate Macaroon Cookies

1 (4-ounce) package sweet baking chocolate
2 egg whites
½ cup sugar
¼ teaspoon vanilla extract
1 (7-ounce) can flaked coconut

Melt chocolate in a heavy saucepan over low heat, stirring occasionally. Remove from heat and cool.

Beat egg whites at high speed of an electric mixer 1 minute. Gradually add sugar, 1 tablespoon at a time, beating until stiff peaks form and sugar dissolves (2 to 4 minutes). Fold in melted chocolate and vanilla; stir in coconut.

Drop mixture by teaspoonfuls onto cookie sheets lined with aluminum foil. Bake at 350° for 12 to 15 minutes. Transfer cookies, leaving them on foil, to wire racks; cool. Carefully remove cookies from foil. **Yield: 4½ dozen.**

Benne Seed Cookies

½ cup butter, melted
1 cup firmly packed brown sugar
1 large egg, beaten
¾ cup all-purpose flour
¼ teaspoon baking powder
½ teaspoon salt
1 teaspoon vanilla extract
1 cup sesame seeds, toasted

Combine all ingredients in a large bowl; beat at medium speed of an electric mixer until smooth.

Drop dough by ½ teaspoonfuls onto lightly greased cookie sheets. Bake at 350° for 8 to 10 minutes or until edges are browned. Cool slightly on cookie sheets, and remove to wire racks. **Yield: 8 dozen.**

Cashew Crunch Cookies

1 cup butter or margarine, softened
¾ cup firmly packed light brown sugar
½ cup sugar
1 large egg
1 teaspoon vanilla extract
2¼ cups all-purpose flour
½ teaspoon baking soda
½ teaspoon cream of tartar
1½ cups finely chopped cashews

Beat butter at medium speed of an electric mixer; gradually add sugars, mixing well. Add egg and vanilla; beat well.

Combine flour, soda, and cream of tartar; gradually add to creamed mixture, mixing after each addition. Stir in cashews.

Drop dough by rounded teaspoonfuls onto lightly greased cookie sheets. Bake at 350° for 10 to 12 minutes or until lightly browned. **Yield: 7 dozen.**

Frosted Apricot Cookies

½ cup butter or margarine, softened
1 (3-ounce) package cream cheese, softened
1¼ cups all-purpose flour
¼ cup sugar
1 teaspoon baking powder
½ cup apricot preserves
½ cup chopped pecans
Apricot Frosting

Beat butter and cream cheese at medium speed of an electric mixer until fluffy.

Combine flour, sugar, and baking powder; stir into creamed mixture. Add apricot preserves and pecans, mixing well.

Drop dough by tablespoonfuls onto greased cookie sheets. Bake at 350° for 12 to 15 minutes. Cool slightly on wire racks. Spread with Apricot Frosting while warm. **Yield: about 3½ dozen.**

Apricot Frosting

1 cup sifted powdered sugar
1 tablespoon butter or margarine, softened
¼ cup apricot preserves

Combine all ingredients, and beat until smooth. **Yield: about ½ cup.**

Sour Cream-Nutmeg Cookies

½ cup butter or margarine, softened
1 cup firmly packed brown sugar
1 large egg
½ cup sour cream
1 cup all-purpose flour
1 cup sifted cake flour
2 teaspoons baking powder
½ teaspoon baking soda
½ teaspoon salt
½ teaspoon ground nutmeg
1 cup chopped pecans

Beat butter at medium speed of an electric mixer until creamy; gradually add sugar, beating well. Add egg and sour cream, and beat well.

Combine all-purpose flour and next 5 ingredients; add to creamed mixture, beating well. Stir in pecans.

Drop dough by heaping teaspoonfuls onto lightly greased cookie sheets. Bake at 350° for 8 to 10 minutes. Cool slightly on cookie sheets; remove to wire racks. **Yield: 5 dozen.**

Apple-Oatmeal Cookies

Apple-Oatmeal Cookies

1 cup all-purpose flour
1 teaspoon baking soda
½ teaspoon salt
1 cup quick-cooking oats, uncooked
½ cup firmly packed brown sugar
1 teaspoon ground cinnamon
¼ teaspoon ground nutmeg
1 large egg
½ cup vegetable oil
1 teaspoon vanilla extract
1 cup peeled, shredded apple (1 medium)
½ cup raisins
⅓ cup chopped pecans

Combine first 7 ingredients in a large bowl, mixing well. Combine egg, oil, and vanilla; stir into dry ingredients. Stir in apple, raisins, and pecans.

Drop dough by rounded teaspoonfuls onto greased cookie sheets. Bake at 350° for 10 to 12 minutes or until lightly browned. Carefully transfer to wire racks to cool. **Yield: 4 dozen.**

Carrot Cookies

½ cup shortening
½ cup butter or margarine, melted
¾ cup sugar
2 large eggs
1¼ cups cooked, mashed carrot
2 cups all-purpose flour
2 teaspoons baking powder
¼ teaspoon salt
1 cup flaked coconut
½ cup chopped pecans

Combine first 3 ingredients in a large mixing bowl; beat at medium speed of an electric mixer until fluffy. Add eggs and carrot, mixing well.

Combine flour, baking powder, and salt; add to creamed mixture, and stir well. Stir in coconut and pecans.

Drop dough by teaspoonfuls onto greased cookie sheets. Bake at 400° for 10 minutes or until firm. Cool on wire racks. **Yield: about 7 dozen.**

Toasted Oat-Coconut Cookies

(pictured on page 43)

¼ cup butter or margarine, softened
¼ cup shortening
1 cup sugar
1 large egg
½ teaspoon coconut extract
1½ cups all-purpose flour
1 teaspoon baking powder
½ teaspoon baking soda
½ teaspoon salt
1 cup flaked coconut
½ cup crispy rice cereal
½ cup pan-toasted or regular oats, uncooked

Beat softened butter and shortening at medium speed of an electric mixer until fluffy; gradually add sugar, beating well. Add egg and coconut extract; beat well.

Combine flour, baking powder, soda, and salt; stir well. Gradually add to creamed mixture, mixing well. Stir in coconut, cereal, and oats.

Drop dough by heaping teaspoonfuls onto lightly greased cookie sheets. Bake at 325° for 12 to 14 minutes or until golden. Let cool slightly on cookie sheets; remove to wire racks to cool completely. **Yield: 4 dozen.**

Mincemeat Drop Cookies

½ cup shortening
½ cup sugar
1 large egg
1 cup prepared mincemeat
1½ cups all-purpose flour
½ teaspoon baking soda
¼ teaspoon salt

Beat shortening at medium speed of an electric mixer until fluffy; gradually add sugar, beating well. Add egg, and beat well. Add mincemeat, mixing well.

Combine flour, soda, and salt; stir into creamed mixture.

Drop dough by teaspoonfuls onto greased cookie sheets. Bake at 350° for 16 to 18 minutes. Cool on wire racks. **Yield: 4½ dozen.**

Crispy-Chewy Molasses Cookies

1 cup butter or margarine
2½ cups sugar
1 teaspoon ground cinnamon
1 teaspoon ground nutmeg
¼ teaspoon salt
1 large egg
¼ cup plus 1 tablespoon water
1 teaspoon baking soda
¼ cup molasses
3½ cups all-purpose flour

Melt butter; cool to room temperature. Combine butter and next 5 ingredients in a large mixing bowl; beat well at medium speed of an electric mixer.

Combine water and soda in a small bowl, stirring until soda dissolves; add soda mixture to creamed mixture, beating well. Stir in molasses and flour.

Drop dough by teaspoonfuls, 3 inches apart, onto greased cookie sheets. Bake at 350° for 7 to 9 minutes. Cool completely on wire racks. **Yield: 8 dozen.**

Oatmeal-Carrot Cookies

1¼ cups butter or margarine, softened
¾ cup firmly packed brown sugar
½ cup sugar
1 large egg
1 teaspoon vanilla extract
1½ cups all-purpose flour
1 teaspoon baking soda
½ teaspoon salt
1 teaspoon ground cinnamon
2 cups regular oats, uncooked
1 cup grated carrot
1 cup chopped pecans

Beat butter at medium speed of an electric mixer until creamy; gradually add sugars, beating well. Add egg and vanilla, mixing well.

Combine flour and next 3 ingredients; add to creamed mixture, mixing well. Stir in oats, carrot, and pecans.

Drop dough by level tablespoonfuls onto ungreased cookie sheets.

Bake at 350° for 10 minutes. Remove cookies to wire racks to cool. Store in an airtight container up to 3 weeks, or freeze up to 8 months. **Yield: 4 dozen.**

Raisin Cookies

2 cups raisins
1 cup water
1 cup shortening
1¾ cups sugar
2 large eggs
1 teaspoon vanilla extract
3½ cups all-purpose flour
1 teaspoon baking powder
1 teaspoon baking soda
½ teaspoon salt
½ teaspoon ground cinnamon
½ teaspoon ground nutmeg
1 cup chopped pecans or walnuts

Combine raisins and water in a medium saucepan; bring to a boil, and boil about 3 minutes. Cool. (Do not drain.)

Beat shortening at medium speed of an electric mixer until fluffy; gradually add sugar, beating well. Add eggs; beat well. Stir in raisins (with liquid) and vanilla.

Combine flour and next 5 ingredients; gradually add to raisin mixture, stirring after each addition. Stir in pecans.

Drop dough by teaspoonfuls 2 inches apart onto well-greased cookie sheets. Bake at 375° for 10 to 12 minutes or until browned. Cool on wire racks. (Cookies will be soft.) **Yield: 5 dozen.**

Walnut Spice Kisses

¼ cup sugar
1 teaspoon ground cinnamon
⅛ teaspoon ground nutmeg
1 egg white
Pinch of salt
1 cup finely chopped walnuts

Combine sugar, cinnamon, and nutmeg, and set aside.

Beat egg white and salt at high speed of an electric mixer 1 minute. Gradually add sugar mixture, 1 tablespoon at a time, beating until stiff peaks form. Fold in walnuts.

Drop mixture by teaspoonfuls onto lightly greased cookie sheets. Bake at 250° for 35 to 40 minutes. **Yield: 2½ dozen.**

Salted Peanut Cookies

1 cup shortening
2 cups firmly packed brown sugar
2 large eggs
2 cups all-purpose flour
1 teaspoon baking powder
1 teaspoon baking soda
½ teaspoon salt
2 cups quick-cooking oats, uncooked
1 cup crispy rice cereal
1 cup salted peanuts

Beat shortening at medium speed of an electric mixer until fluffy; gradually add sugar, beating well. Add eggs, and beat well.

Combine flour, baking powder, soda, and salt; add to creamed mixture, mixing well. Stir in oats, cereal, and peanuts. (Dough will be stiff.)

Drop dough by rounded teaspoonfuls onto lightly greased cookie sheets. Bake at 375° for 10 to 12 minutes. Remove cookies to wire racks to cool. **Yield: 7 dozen.**

Granola Cookies

Combine flour and next 3 ingredients; add to creamed mixture, mixing well. Stir in granola and raisins.

Drop dough by rounded tablespoonfuls onto lightly greased cookie sheets.

Bake at 375° for 10 to 12 minutes or until lightly browned. Cool 1 minute on cookie sheets; remove to wire racks to cool completely. **Yield: 4½ dozen.**

Take-Along Breakfast Cookies

¾ cup all-purpose flour
½ teaspoon baking soda
½ teaspoon salt
⅔ cup butter or margarine, softened
⅔ cup sugar
1 large egg
1 teaspoon vanilla extract
1½ cups regular oats, uncooked
1 cup (4 ounces) shredded Cheddar cheese
½ cup wheat germ
6 slices bacon, cooked and crumbled

Combine flour, soda, and salt; mix well, and set aside.

Beat butter and sugar at medium speed of an electric mixer until fluffy; add egg and vanilla, beating well. Add flour mixture, mixing well. Stir in oats, cheese, wheat germ, and bacon.

Drop dough by rounded tablespoonfuls onto ungreased cookie sheets. Bake at 350° for 14 to 16 minutes. Cool 1 minute on cookie sheets. **Yield: 2 dozen.**

Granola Cookies

1 cup butter or margarine, softened
¾ cup firmly packed brown sugar
½ cup sugar
1 large egg
1 teaspoon vanilla extract
1½ cups all-purpose flour
1 teaspoon baking soda
½ teaspoon salt
1 teaspoon ground cinnamon
4 cups commercial granola
½ cup raisins

Beat butter at medium speed of an electric mixer until creamy; gradually add sugars, beating well. Add egg and vanilla, mixing well.

Cookie Tip

Keep a batch of either one of these cookies on hand for a quick early morning break. Grab a bite on the run or pack a few to have as a mid-morning snack.

Refrigerator Specialties

Enjoy the convenience of storing dough for sliced or rolled cookies in the refrigerator. At a moment's notice, you can have the aroma of freshly baked cookies drifting through the house.

Golden Sugar Cookies, Almond Biscotti, Memory Book Cookies

Dainty Sandwich Cookies, Strawberry Cookie Tarts, Gingerbirds, Biscochitos

Vanilla Slice-and-Bake Cookies, Crispy Shortbread Cookies, Chocolate-Mint Swirls

Moravian Sugar Cookies, Grandma's Tea Cakes, Snowflake Cookies

Sugar Cookie Cutouts (page 74)

Golden Sugar Cookies

1 cup butter or margarine, softened
½ cup sugar
1 large egg
1 teaspoon lemon extract
2¼ cups all-purpose flour
1½ teaspoons baking powder
½ teaspoon salt
1 tablespoon whipping cream or half-and-half
Red and green decorator sugar crystals

Beat butter at medium speed of an electric mixer until creamy; gradually add ½ cup sugar, beating well. Add egg, beating well. Stir in lemon extract.

Combine flour, baking powder, and salt; add to creamed mixture, beating well. Shape dough into two 12-inch rolls; wrap in wax paper, and chill at least 6 hours.

Unwrap rolls, and cut into ¼-inch slices; place on lightly greased cookie sheets. Brush tops of cookies with cream, and sprinkle evenly with sugar crystals.

Bake at 400° for 8 minutes. Cool on wire racks. **Yield: 6 dozen.**

Note: Dough may be frozen by wrapping securely and freezing up to 1 month. Remove from freezer; slice dough, and bake as directed.

Vanilla Slice-and-Bake Cookies

½ cup butter or margarine, softened
1 cup sugar
1 large egg
2 teaspoons vanilla extract
1¾ cups all-purpose flour
½ teaspoon baking soda
¼ teaspoon salt
½ cup chopped pecans

Beat butter at medium speed of an electric mixer until creamy; gradually add sugar, beating well. Add egg and vanilla; beat well.

Combine flour, soda, and salt; add to creamed mixture, beating well. Stir in pecans. Shape dough into two 12-inch rolls; wrap in wax paper, and chill at least 2 hours.

Unwrap rolls, and cut into ¼-inch slices; place on ungreased cookie sheets. Bake at 350° for 10 to 12 minutes. Cool slightly; remove to wire racks to cool completely. **Yield: about 7 dozen.**

Variation

Slice of Spice Cookies: Prepare Vanilla Slice-and-Bake Cookies, substituting firmly packed brown sugar for sugar. Combine ¼ cup granulated sugar and 2 teaspoons ground cinnamon; dip each slice in mixture before baking.

Note: Dough may be frozen up to 3 months. Slice dough while frozen, and bake as directed.

Crispy Shortbread Cookies

½ cup butter or margarine, softened
½ cup shortening
1½ cups sifted powdered sugar
1½ teaspoons vanilla extract
1¼ cups all-purpose flour
1½ cups cornflakes
½ cup finely chopped pecans

Beat butter and shortening at medium speed of an electric mixer until fluffy; gradually add sugar, beating until smooth. Add vanilla and flour, beating well. Stir in cornflakes.

Shape dough into a long roll, 2 inches in diameter; gently roll in pecans. Wrap in wax paper, and chill 8 hours or until firm.

Let roll stand at room temperature about 10 minutes. Cut dough into ¼-inch slices; place 2 inches apart on ungreased cookie sheets.

Bake at 350° for 15 minutes or until lightly browned. Cool on wire racks. **Yield: 3½ dozen.**

Ginger Icebox Cookies

1 cup butter **or margarine, softened**
1 cup sugar
4½ cups **all-purpose flour**
1 teaspoon **baking soda**
1 teaspoon **ground ginger**
1 teaspoon **ground cinnamon**
1 cup **molasses**
¼ cup **water**

Beat butter at medium speed of an electric mixer until creamy; gradually add sugar, beating mixture well.

Combine flour and next 3 ingredients; add to creamed mixture alternately with molasses and water. (Dough will be very soft.) Cover and chill 2 hours.

Divide dough into 4 equal portions; shape into 9-inch rolls, and wrap each in wax paper. Freeze at least 2 hours.

Unwrap rolls, and cut into ¼-inch slices; place on lightly greased cookie sheets.

Bake at 350° for 10 to 12 minutes. Cool 3 minutes on cookie sheets. Transfer to wire racks to cool completely. **Yield: 10 dozen.**

Ginger Icebox Cookies

Memory Book Cookies

1 cup butter **or margarine, softened**
2 cups **firmly packed brown sugar**
2 large **eggs**
1 teaspoon **vanilla extract**
3½ cups **all-purpose flour**
1 teaspoon **baking soda**
½ teaspoon **salt**
1 cup **chopped pecans**

Beat butter at medium speed of an electric mixer until creamy; gradually add sugar, beating well. Add eggs and vanilla; mix well.

Combine flour, soda, and salt; gradually add to creamed mixture, mixing well. Stir in pecans. Shape dough into two 16-inch rolls; wrap in wax paper, and chill at least 4 hours.

Unwrap rolls, and cut into ⅓-inch slices; place on ungreased cookie sheets. Bake at 375° for 6 to 8 minutes. Cool on wire racks. **Yield: 8 dozen.**

Note: Dough may be frozen up to 3 months. Slice dough while frozen, and bake as directed.

Memory Book Cookies

Valentine Sugar Cookies

¾ cup shortening
1 cup sugar
2 large eggs
1 teaspoon vanilla extract
2½ cups all-purpose flour
1 teaspoon baking powder
½ teaspoon salt
Decorator Frosting

Beat shortening at medium speed of an electric mixer until fluffy; gradually add sugar, beating well. Add eggs and vanilla; mix well.

Combine flour, baking powder, and salt; add to creamed mixture, mixing well. Divide dough in half; wrap in wax paper, and chill at least 1 hour.

Roll half of dough to ¼-inch thickness on a lightly floured surface; keep remaining dough chilled. Cut dough with a heart-shaped cookie cutter. Place on lightly greased cookie sheets.

Bake at 350° for 12 minutes or until edges are lightly browned. Cool cookies on a wire rack. Repeat with remaining dough. Spread with Decorator Frosting. **Yield: 3 dozen.**

Decorator Frosting

¼ cup plus 2 tablespoons butter or
     margarine, softened
1 (16-ounce) package powdered sugar, sifted
¼ cup milk
1 teaspoon vanilla extract
Red liquid food coloring (optional)

Beat butter at medium speed of an electric mixer until creamy; gradually add sugar, beating until well blended. Add milk and vanilla, mixing until smooth. Stir in food coloring, if desired. **Yield: frosting for 3 dozen cookies.**

Valentine Butter Cookies

½ cup butter, softened
½ cup shortening
1 cup sugar
3 large eggs
3½ cups all-purpose flour
2 teaspoons cream of tartar
1 teaspoon baking soda
1½ teaspoons vanilla extract
Red decorator sugar crystals

Beat butter and shortening at medium speed of an electric mixer until fluffy; gradually add sugar, beating well. Add eggs, one at a time, beating after each addition.

Combine flour, cream of tartar, and soda; add to creamed mixture, beating well. Stir in vanilla. Cover and chill 2 hours.

Work with half of dough at a time; store remainder in refrigerator. Roll dough on a lightly floured surface to ¼-inch thickness; cut with a heart-shaped cookie cutter. Place on ungreased cookie sheets. Sprinkle cookies with decorator sugar crystals.

Bake at 425° for 6 to 8 minutes or until lightly browned. Store in airtight containers, placing wax paper between layers of cookies. **Yield: about 5½ dozen.**

Decorating Tip

When frosting cookies, occasionally dip the knife or spatula in warm water to smooth out the frosting.

Grandma's Tea Cakes

Grandma's Tea Cakes

1 cup shortening
1½ cups sugar
3 large eggs
4 cups all-purpose flour
2 teaspoons baking powder
1 teaspoon baking soda
½ teaspoon salt
¼ cup buttermilk
1 to 1¼ teaspoons almond extract
Sugar (optional)

Beat shortening at medium speed of an electric mixer until fluffy; gradually add 1½ cups sugar, beating well. Add eggs, one at a time, beating after each addition.

Combine flour and next 3 ingredients; add to creamed mixture alternately with buttermilk. Mix well. Stir in extract. Cover and chill 1 hour.

Roll dough to ¼-inch thickness on a floured surface. Cut with a 2¾-inch round cookie cutter; place on greased cookie sheets.

Bake at 350° for 15 minutes or until edges begin to brown. Sprinkle with sugar, if desired.
Yield: 4 dozen.

Dainty Sandwich Cookies

(pictured on page 2)

1 cup butter, softened
⅔ cup sugar
2 egg yolks
2½ cups all-purpose flour
¼ teaspoon salt
1 to 2 tablespoons powdered sugar
½ cup sugar
½ cup ground blanched almonds
2 egg whites
About 1½ cups raspberry preserves
Powdered sugar (optional)
½ cup semisweet chocolate morsels, melted

Beat butter at medium speed of an electric mixer until creamy; gradually add ⅔ cup sugar, beating well. Add egg yolks, one at a time, beating well.

Combine flour and salt; add to creamed mixture, beating well. Shape dough into a ball; cover and chill at least 2 hours.

Divide dough in half; store 1 portion in refrigerator. Sift powdered sugar lightly over work surface. Roll half of dough to ⅛-inch thickness; cut with a 2½-inch round cutter. Roll remaining dough as before; cut with a 2½-inch doughnut cutter, reserving centers.

Combine ½ cup sugar and almonds; mix well. Beat egg whites until frothy. Brush one side of all cookie cutouts with egg white, and coat with almond mixture; place coated side up on lightly greased cookie sheets.

Bake at 375° for 8 to 10 minutes or until lightly browned. Cool on wire racks. Repeat procedure with remaining dough.

Assemble cookies according to the following directions.

Raspberry Sandwich Cookies: Spread uncoated side of each solid cookie with a thin layer of raspberry preserves. (Cookies are very delicate and must be handled carefully.) Lightly dust almond side of doughnut-shaped cookies with powdered sugar, if desired; place sugar side up on top of raspberry filling. **Yield: 2 dozen.**

Chocolate Sandwich Cookies: Using half of reserved cookie centers, spread a thin layer of melted chocolate on side without almonds. Top with remaining cookie centers, almond side up. Drizzle tops of cookies with remaining chocolate, if desired. **Yield: 1 dozen.**

Snowflake Cookies

1 cup butter or margarine, softened
½ cup sugar
2 tablespoons milk
1 tablespoon lemon rind
½ teaspoon vanilla extract
¼ teaspoon lemon extract
2½ cups all-purpose flour
Sifted powdered sugar

Beat butter at medium speed of an electric mixer until creamy; gradually add sugar, beating well.

Stir in milk, lemon rind, and flavorings. Gradually add flour, mixing after each addition.

Roll dough to ⅛-inch thickness on an ungreased cookie sheet; cut close together with a 2-inch round cookie cutter. Carefully remove excess dough from cookie sheet. Using a drinking straw, randomly cut holes in dough, removing dough by slightly twisting straw.

Bake at 375° for 6 to 7 minutes. (Cookies will not brown.) Remove cookies to wire racks to cool. Sprinkle with powdered sugar. **Yield: 6 dozen.**

Note: Freeze cookies in airtight containers up to six months.

Oat Crispies

1½ cups all-purpose flour
1½ cups regular oats, uncooked
½ cup sugar
¾ teaspoon salt
½ teaspoon baking soda
¾ cup butter or margarine, softened
2 to 4 tablespoons cold water

Combine first 5 ingredients in a large bowl; cut in butter with a pastry blender until crumbly. Sprinkle cold water evenly over surface; stir with a fork until dry ingredients are moistened.

Roll dough to ¼-inch thickness on a lightly floured surface; cut into rounds with a 2-inch cutter.

Place cookies on a lightly greased cookie sheet; bake at 350° for 15 minutes. Remove cookies to wire racks to cool. **Yield: 3½ dozen.**

Strawberry Cookie Tarts

⅓ cup shortening
⅓ cup sugar
1 large egg
1 teaspoon vanilla extract
1 cup all-purpose flour
1 teaspoon baking powder
½ teaspoon salt
1 egg white, lightly beaten
¼ cup red currant jelly
2 teaspoons water
1 pint fresh strawberries, sliced

Beat shortening at medium speed of an electric mixer until fluffy; add sugar, beating well. Add egg and vanilla, and beat until blended.

Combine flour, baking powder, and salt; stir into creamed mixture, mixing well. Cover and chill at least 3 hours.

Roll dough to ⅛-inch thickness between two sheets of wax paper. Remove top sheet of wax paper. Cut dough with a 4- x 3-inch wedge-shaped cookie cutter, removing excess dough. Transfer cookies on wax paper to a cookie sheet. Freeze 15 minutes. Remove cookies from wax paper, and place on a lightly greased cookie sheet. Repeat procedure with remaining dough.

Brush cookies with beaten egg white. Bake at 375° for 10 to 12 minutes or until lightly browned. Cool on wire racks.

Combine red currant jelly and water in a small saucepan; cook over low heat until jelly melts, stirring constantly. Cool slightly.

Brush cookies with jelly mixture; arrange

strawberry slices, slightly overlapping, on cookies. Brush strawberries with jelly mixture. **Yield: 1 dozen.**

Biscochitos

2 cups shortening
1 cup sugar
2 large eggs
1 teaspoon anise seeds, crushed
5½ cups all-purpose flour
1 tablespoon baking powder
1 teaspoon salt
¼ cup white wine or dry sherry
½ cup sugar
1 teaspoon ground cinnamon

Beat shortening at medium speed of electric mixer until fluffy; gradually add 1 cup sugar, and beat well. Add eggs and anise seeds; mix well.

Combine flour, baking powder, and salt; add to creamed mixture alternately with wine, beginning and ending with flour mixture. Mix after each addition.

Shape dough into a ball; roll to ¼-inch thickness on a floured surface. Cut dough with a 3-inch cookie cutter, and place on lightly greased cookie sheets. Combine ½ cup sugar and cinnamon; sprinkle over cookies.

Bake at 350° for 8 to 10 minutes or until lightly browned. Transfer to wire racks to cool. **Yield: about 6 dozen.**

Italian Cinnamon Sticks

¾ cup sugar
½ cup walnuts, ground
1 teaspoon ground cinnamon
1 cup butter or margarine, softened
1 (8-ounce) package cream cheese, softened
2½ cups all-purpose flour
1 large egg, lightly beaten

Combine first 3 ingredients in a small bowl; set aside.

Beat butter and cream cheese at medium speed of an electric mixer until creamy; gradually add flour, mixing until well blended. Shape dough into a ball; wrap in plastic wrap, and chill 30 minutes.

Divide dough in half; place 1 portion between 2 sheets of lightly floured wax paper, and roll dough into a 10-inch square (about ⅛ inch thick). Brush with egg; sprinkle with half of sugar mixture.

Cut dough into 5- x ½-inch strips; twist and place on ungreased baking sheets. Repeat procedure with remaining dough and sugar mixture.

Bake at 350° for 10 to 12 minutes or until golden. Remove to wire racks to cool. **Yield: about 6½ dozen.**

Tips for Cutout Cookies

When you're in a hurry and don't have time to cut rolled dough with cookie cutters, cut the dough into squares or diamonds, using a sharp knife, fluted pastry wheel, or pizza cutter. This eliminates most scraps, too.

If you have extra time but lack the cutter shape you want, cut your own patterns from cardboard or sturdy construction paper. Lay the pattern on the rolled dough, and trim around it with a sharp knife.

Watermelon Cookies

Watermelon Cookies

⅓ cup butter or margarine, softened
⅓ cup shortening
¾ cup sugar
1 large egg
1 tablespoon milk
1 teaspoon vanilla extract
2 cups all-purpose flour
1½ teaspoons baking powder
½ teaspoon salt
Red paste food coloring
⅓ cup semisweet chocolate mini-morsels
1½ cups sifted powdered sugar
2 tablespoons water
Green paste food coloring

Beat butter and shortening at medium speed of an electric mixer until fluffy; gradually add sugar, beating well. Stir in egg, milk, and vanilla.

Combine flour, baking powder, and salt; gradually add to creamed mixture, mixing well. Add a small amount of red food coloring to color dough as desired, beating until blended. Shape dough into a ball; cover and chill at least 3 hours.

Divide dough in half; store one portion in refrigerator. Roll remaining portion to ¼-inch thickness on a lightly floured surface.

Cut dough with a 3-inch round cookie cutter; cut circle in half. Place on an ungreased cookie sheet. Press several chocolate mini-morsels in each cookie. Repeat with remaining dough.

Bake at 375° for 8 to 10 minutes (do not brown). Cool on wire racks.

Combine powdered sugar and water, mixing until smooth. Add a small amount of green food coloring, mixing until blended. Dip round edge of each cookie in green frosting, and place cookie on wax paper until frosting is firm. **Yield: 3 dozen.**

Note: You can purchase paste food coloring at specialty shops, bakery supply stores, or craft stores.

Watermelon Cookies Techniques

Cut dough with round cookie cutter; then slice rounds in half, and transfer to cookie sheets.

Press three or four chocolate mini-morsels into each unbaked cookie to look like seeds.

After cookies have cooled, dip rounded edge of each cookie into green frosting to simulate watermelon rind.

Gingerbirds

electric mixer until butter melts. Cool 10 minutes.

Add eggs; beat at low speed until blended. Gradually add flour, mixing after each addition. Divide dough in half; wrap each portion in plastic wrap, and chill 30 minutes.

Roll each portion to ¼-inch thickness on a lightly floured surface. Cut with a 4- or 5-inch, bird-shaped cutter, and place on lightly greased cookie sheets.

Bake at 325° for 12 minutes or until firm to touch. Transfer to wire racks to cool.

Spread a thin layer of Yellow Decorator Frosting on cookies; add nonpareils for eyes. Let dry. Store in an airtight container. **Yield: 6 dozen (4-inch) or 3½ dozen (5-inch) cookies.**

Gingerbirds

1 cup molasses
½ cup sugar
½ cup firmly packed brown sugar
1 tablespoon ground ginger
1 tablespoon ground cinnamon
½ teaspoon ground cloves
2¼ teaspoons baking soda
1 cup butter or margarine, softened
2 large eggs
6 cups all-purpose flour
Yellow Decorator Frosting
Nonpareils

Combine first 6 ingredients in top of a double boiler; place over boiling water, and cook, stirring constantly, until sugar melts. Stir in soda; remove top of double boiler from heat.

Place butter in a large mixing bowl; add hot molasses mixture, and beat at low speed of an

Yellow Decorator Frosting

4 cups sifted powdered sugar
3 tablespoons lemon juice
3 tablespoons water
Yellow paste food coloring

Combine first 3 ingredients; stir until smooth. Stir in desired amount of food coloring. **Yield: 1½ cups.**

Cookie Tip

Use your microwave oven to soften butter or margarine. Place butter in a microwave-safe bowl, and microwave at LOW (10% power) until softened. For 1 to 2 tablespoons, microwave 15 to 30 seconds; for ¼ to ½ cup, microwave 1 to 1¼ minutes; and for 1 cup, microwave 1¾ minutes.

Of Bars and Squares

Whether you prefer moist, chewy brownies or fancy cakelike squares, this assortment of bar cookies is deliciously simple—and simply delicious.

Almond-Chocolate Bars, Butter Pecan Turtle Bars, Granola Bars

Amaretto Brownies, Cream Cheese Swirl Brownies, Blonde Chocolate Chip Brownies

Lemon Hearts, Peanut Butter Bars, German Chocolate Chess Squares, By-Cracky Bars

Macadamia-Fudge Designer Brownies, Frosted Blonde Brownies

Mississippi Mud Brownies (page 88)

Brownie Mix

7 cups sugar
4 cups all-purpose flour
2½ cups cocoa
1 tablespoon plus 1 teaspoon baking powder
1 tablespoon salt
2 cups shortening

Combine first 5 ingredients; stir well. Cut in shortening with a pastry blender until mixture is crumbly.

Place in an airtight container; store in a cool, dry place or in refrigerator up to 6 weeks. **Yield: 14 cups.**

Quick and Easy Brownies

3 cups Brownie Mix
½ cup chopped pecans
3 large eggs, beaten
1½ teaspoons vanilla extract

Combine all ingredients, stirring until blended. Spoon into a greased and floured 8-inch square pan.

Bake at 350° for 35 to 40 minutes. Cool and cut into squares. **Yield: 16 brownies.**

Biscuit Mix Brownies

1 (12-ounce) package semisweet chocolate
    morsels
¼ cup butter or margarine
1 (14-ounce) can sweetened condensed milk
1 large egg, lightly beaten
2 cups biscuit mix
1½ cups chopped pecans
1 (16-ounce) container ready-to-spread
    chocolate fudge frosting (optional)

Combine chocolate morsels and butter in a microwave-safe bowl; microwave at HIGH 2 minutes, stirring once.

Stir in condensed milk and next 3 ingredients. Spoon into a greased 13- x 9- x 2-inch pan.

Bake at 350° for 25 to 30 minutes. Cool slightly on a wire rack. Spread chocolate frosting on warm brownies, if desired. Cut into squares. **Yield: 3 dozen.**

Quick Brownies

½ cup chopped pecans
2 (1-ounce) squares unsweetened chocolate
½ cup butter or margarine, cut into 4 pieces
1 teaspoon instant coffee granules
1 cup firmly packed light brown sugar
2 large eggs, beaten
1 teaspoon vanilla extract
⅔ cup all-purpose flour
½ teaspoon baking powder
Frosting

Spread chopped pecans in a pieplate. Microwave at HIGH 3 to 3½ minutes. Set aside.

Place chocolate and butter in a microwave-safe bowl. Microwave at MEDIUM (50% power) 2½ minutes or until chocolate melts, stirring at 1-minute intervals.

Stir coffee granules into chocolate mixture. Add sugar, and stir until blended. Add eggs and vanilla, mixing well. Stir in pecans, flour, and baking powder.

Spread mixture into a greased and floured 8-inch square baking dish; shield corners with triangles of aluminum foil, keeping foil smooth and close to dish. Place dish on top of a microwave-safe cereal bowl inverted in oven.

Microwave at MEDIUM 8 minutes, giving dish a quarter-turn at 4-minute intervals. Remove foil from corners.

Microwave at HIGH 1 to 2 minutes or until a wooden pick inserted in center comes out clean. Place directly on counter, and let stand 20 minutes. Spread frosting over brownies. Cut into squares, and immediately remove from dish. **Yield: 16 brownies.**

Frosting

1 (1-ounce) square unsweetened chocolate
1 tablespoon butter or margarine
1 cup sifted powdered sugar
Dash of ground cinnamon
Dash of salt
1 to 2 tablespoons milk
½ teaspoon vanilla extract

Place unsweetened chocolate and butter in a small microwave-safe bowl. Microwave at MEDIUM (50% power) 1½ to 2 minutes or until chocolate melts, stirring at 1-minute intervals.

Stir in powdered sugar, cinnamon, and salt. Add milk and vanilla, stirring until mixture is smooth. **Yield: ½ cup.**

Cutting Bar Cookies

Bar cookies may be cut into various sizes and shapes. The yield of each recipe depends on the size of the pan as well as the size of the serving. Usually the thicker or richer the bar, the smaller it should be cut. You can adjust the yield of each recipe by cutting larger or smaller portions.

Besides cutting into bars and squares, bar cookies may be cut into diamond shapes. To do so, cut diagonally in one direction and straight across in the other direction. The yield will be slightly less.

Easy Frosted Brownies

(pictured on page 2)

½ cup sugar
⅓ cup butter or margarine
2 tablespoons water
1 (6-ounce) package semisweet chocolate
    morsels
1 teaspoon vanilla extract
2 large eggs
¾ cup all-purpose flour
¼ teaspoon baking soda
¼ teaspoon salt
1 cup chopped pecans or walnuts
1 (6-ounce) package semisweet chocolate
    morsels (optional)
½ cup chopped pecans or walnuts (optional)

Combine first 3 ingredients in a medium saucepan; cook over high heat, stirring frequently, until mixture comes to a boil. Remove mixture from heat.

Add 1 package chocolate morsels and vanilla, stirring until chocolate melts. Add eggs, one at a time, beating after each addition.

Combine flour, soda, and salt; stir dry ingredients and 1 cup pecans into chocolate mixture.

Pour batter into a greased and floured 9-inch square pan. Bake at 325° for 30 minutes. Cool on a wire rack.

Cut brownies into squares and serve plain, or sprinkle 1 package chocolate morsels over hot brownies, if desired. Let stand until morsels are softened; then spread evenly over brownies with a spatula. Sprinkle ½ cup pecans on top, if desired. Cool and cut into squares. **Yield: 3 dozen.**

Buttermilk Cake Brownies

½ cup butter or margarine
½ cup cocoa
1 cup water
½ cup vegetable oil
2 cups all-purpose flour
2 cups sugar
¼ teaspoon salt
½ cup buttermilk
2 large eggs, beaten
1 teaspoon baking soda
1 teaspoon vanilla extract
Chocolate Frosting

Combine first 3 ingredients in a small saucepan; cook over medium heat, stirring frequently, until mixture comes to a boil. Remove from heat. Stir in oil.

Combine flour, sugar, and salt in a large bowl; add cocoa mixture, stirring well. Stir in buttermilk, eggs, soda, and vanilla.

Pour batter into a greased and floured 13- x 9- x 2-inch pan. Bake at 350° for 30 minutes. Spread with Chocolate Frosting while warm. Cool and cut into squares. **Yield: 2 dozen.**

Chocolate Frosting

½ cup butter or margarine, softened
½ cup cocoa
¼ cup plus 2 tablespoons hot water
1 teaspoon vanilla extract
1 (16-ounce) package powdered sugar, sifted
1 cup chopped pecans (optional)

Combine first 4 ingredients; blend until smooth. Gradually add powdered sugar, mixing well. Stir in chopped pecans, if desired. **Yield: enough frosting for 2 dozen brownies.**

Southern Chocolate-Mint Brownies

4 large eggs
2 cups sugar
1 cup all-purpose flour
1 cup cocoa
1 cup butter or margarine, melted
1 teaspoon vanilla extract
½ teaspoon peppermint extract
Mint Cream Frosting
3 (1-ounce) squares unsweetened chocolate
3 tablespoons butter or margarine

Beat eggs lightly with a wire whisk in a large bowl. Add sugar, and stir well.

Combine flour and cocoa; gradually stir into egg mixture. Stir in 1 cup butter and flavorings.

Pour into a greased 15- x 10- x 1-inch jelly-roll pan; bake at 350° for 15 to 18 minutes or until a wooden pick inserted in center comes out clean. Cool in pan on a wire rack.

Spread Mint Cream Frosting over brownie layer; freeze 15 minutes. Melt chocolate squares and 3 tablespoons butter in a heavy saucepan over low heat, stirring constantly, until melted. Spread over frosting with a pastry brush. Chill until firm; cut into squares. Store in refrigerator. **Yield: 2 dozen.**

Mint Cream Frosting

¼ cup butter or margarine, softened
2¾ cups sifted powdered sugar
2 to 3 tablespoons milk
½ teaspoon peppermint extract
3 or 4 drops of green liquid food coloring

Beat butter at medium speed of an electric mixer; gradually add powdered sugar, beating after each addition. Add milk, and beat until mixture is spreading consistency. Stir in peppermint extract and food coloring. **Yield: about 2 cups.**

Southern Chocolate-Mint Brownies

Mississippi Mud Brownies

(pictured on page 83)

4 (1-ounce) squares unsweetened chocolate
1 cup butter or margarine
2 cups sugar
1 cup all-purpose flour
⅛ teaspoon salt
4 large eggs, beaten
1 cup chopped pecans
3 cups miniature marshmallows
Fudge Frosting

Combine chocolate and butter in a large saucepan; cook over low heat, stirring until chocolate and butter melt. Remove from heat.

Combine sugar, flour, and salt; add to chocolate mixture. Add eggs and pecans; stir until blended. Spoon batter into a lightly greased and floured 13- x 9- x 2-inch pan.

Bake at 350° for 25 to 30 minutes or until a wooden pick inserted in center comes out clean.

Sprinkle marshmallows evenly over hot brownies. Spread with Fudge Frosting. Cool and cut into squares. **Yield: 2 dozen.**

Fudge Frosting

2 (1-ounce) squares unsweetened chocolate
½ cup evaporated milk
½ cup butter or margarine
4½ to 5 cups sifted powdered sugar
½ teaspoon vanilla extract

Combine first 3 ingredients in a heavy saucepan. Cook over low heat, stirring until chocolate and butter melt. Remove from heat. Transfer to a medium bowl. Gradually add powdered sugar and vanilla, beating at low speed of an electric mixer until smooth. **Yield: 2⅓ cups.**

Mississippi Mud Brownies Techniques

Grease and flour pan before baking; this makes baked brownies easy to remove from pan.

Sprinkle marshmallows over hot brownies; marshmallows will soften and cling to brownies.

Pour Fudge Frosting over marshmallows. Quickly spread frosting, smoothing evenly with a spatula.

Triple Decker Brownies

1½ cups quick-cooking oats, toasted
1 cup all-purpose flour
1 cup firmly packed brown sugar
½ teaspoon baking soda
¼ teaspoon salt
¾ cup butter or margarine, melted
2 (1-ounce) squares unsweetened chocolate
½ cup butter or margarine
1½ cups sugar
2 large eggs
1⅓ cups all-purpose flour
½ teaspoon baking powder
¼ teaspoon salt
½ cup milk
1 teaspoon vanilla extract
1 cup chopped pecans
Chocolate Frosting

Combine first 5 ingredients in a large bowl; add ¾ cup melted butter, stirring well.

Press mixture into two greased 8-inch square pans. Bake at 350° for 10 minutes.

Melt chocolate and ½ cup butter in a large, heavy saucepan over low heat; remove from heat. Add sugar and eggs, mixing well.

Combine 1⅓ cups flour, baking powder, and ¼ teaspoon salt; add to chocolate mixture alternately with milk. Stir in vanilla and pecans. Spread over crust.

Bake at 350° for 20 to 25 minutes. Cool on wire racks. Spread with Chocolate Frosting. Cut into 2-inch squares. **Yield: 32 brownies.**

Chocolate Frosting

2 (1-ounce) squares unsweetened chocolate
¼ cup butter or margarine
3 cups sifted powdered sugar
2 teaspoons vanilla extract
3 to 4 tablespoons hot water

Melt chocolate and butter in a large, heavy saucepan over low heat; remove from heat. Stir in powdered sugar, vanilla, and 1 tablespoon water. Stir in additional water until desired spreading consistency. **Yield: 1½ cups.**

Macadamia-Fudge Designer Brownies

2½ cups sugar
1½ cups butter or margarine
5 (1-ounce) squares unsweetened chocolate
6 large eggs, lightly beaten
2 cups all-purpose flour
1 cup coarsely chopped macadamia nuts or almonds
Fudge Frosting
Garnish: chopped macadamia nuts

Combine first 3 ingredients in a large, heavy saucepan; cook over low heat, stirring often, until chocolate melts. Remove from heat, and cool 10 minutes.

Stir in eggs, flour, and 1 cup nuts. Pour into a greased and floured 13- x 9- x 2-inch pan.

Bake at 350° for 30 to 35 minutes. Cool on a wire rack.

Pour Fudge Frosting over top; chill 15 minutes, and cut into squares. Garnish, if desired. **Yield: 4 dozen.**

Fudge Frosting

1 cup whipping cream
12 (1-ounce) squares semisweet chocolate

Heat whipping cream in a medium saucepan over medium heat; add chocolate, stirring until smooth.

Remove from heat, and cool to room temperature. **Yield: 2½ cups.**

Candy Bar Brownies

Candy Bar Brownies

4 large eggs, lightly beaten
2 cups sugar
¾ cup butter or margarine, melted
2 teaspoons vanilla extract
1½ cups all-purpose flour
½ teaspoon baking powder
¼ teaspoon salt
⅓ cup cocoa
4 (2.07-ounce) chocolate-coated caramel-peanut nougat bars, coarsely chopped
3 (1.55-ounce) milk chocolate candy bars, finely chopped

Combine first 4 ingredients in a large bowl. Combine flour and next 3 ingredients; stir into sugar mixture. Fold in chopped nougat bars.

Spoon mixture into a greased and floured 13- x 9- x 2-inch pan; sprinkle with chopped milk chocolate bars. Bake at 350° for 30 to 35 minutes. Cool and cut into squares. **Yield: 2½ dozen.**

Note: For nougat bars, we used Snickers candy bars; for milk chocolate bars, we used Hershey's candy bars.

Candy Bar Tips

• To easily chop chocolate candy bars with nuts and caramel, use a sharp, sturdy knife.
• To quickly crush crunchy chocolate bars, position knife blade in food processor bowl; add chilled candy, and process until crushed.
• To melt milk chocolate candy bars, place in a small, heavy saucepan, and stir over low heat until candy melts. Or place in a small microwave-safe bowl, and microwave at LOW (30% power), stirring often, until candy melts.

Amaretto Brownies

1 cup shortening
4 (1-ounce) squares unsweetened chocolate
2 cups sugar
4 large eggs, beaten
2 tablespoons amaretto or other almond flavored liqueur
1½ cups all-purpose flour
½ teaspoon salt
Amaretto Frosting
3 to 4 tablespoons sliced almonds

Combine shortening and chocolate in a heavy saucepan; place over low heat, stirring constantly, until melted. Add sugar, stirring until combined. Remove from heat and cool. Stir in eggs and amaretto.

Combine flour and salt; add to creamed mixture, stirring well. Pour batter into a lightly greased 13- x 9- x 2-inch pan.

Bake at 400° for 20 minutes; cool. Spread with Amaretto Frosting. Sprinkle with sliced almonds, and cut into squares. **Yield: 2½ dozen.**

Amaretto Frosting

¼ cup butter or margarine
1 (1-ounce) square unsweetened chocolate
2 tablespoons half-and-half
2½ cups sifted powdered sugar
Dash of salt
2 tablespoons amaretto

Combine butter and chocolate in a heavy saucepan; place over low heat, stirring constantly, until melted. Stir in half-and-half.

Add powdered sugar, salt, and amaretto, stirring until smooth. **Yield: enough frosting for 2½ dozen brownies.**

Cream Cheese Swirl Brownies

1 (4-ounce) package sweet baking chocolate
3 tablespoons butter or margarine
2 tablespoons butter or margarine, softened
1 (3-ounce) package cream cheese, softened
¼ cup sugar
1 large egg
1 tablespoon all-purpose flour
½ teaspoon vanilla extract
2 large eggs
¾ cup sugar
½ cup all-purpose flour
½ teaspoon baking powder
¼ teaspoon salt
1 teaspoon vanilla extract
¼ teaspoon almond extract
½ cup chopped pecans or walnuts

Melt chocolate and 3 tablespoons butter in a heavy saucepan over low heat. Set aside to cool.

Beat 2 tablespoons butter and cream cheese at medium speed of an electric mixer until fluffy. Gradually add ¼ cup sugar, beating well. Stir in 1 egg, 1 tablespoon flour, and ½ teaspoon vanilla. Set aside.

Beat 2 eggs at medium speed of an electric mixer until thick and pale. Gradually add ¾ cup sugar, beating well. Combine ½ cup flour, baking powder, and salt; add to egg mixture, mixing well. Stir in cooled chocolate, flavorings, and pecans.

Pour half of chocolate batter into a greased 8-inch square pan. Spread with cream cheese mixture; top with remaining chocolate batter. Cut through mixture in pan with a knife to create a marbled effect.

Bake at 350° for 35 to 40 minutes. Cool on a wire rack; cut into squares. **Yield: 16 brownies.**

Cheesecake Brownies

½ cup butter or margarine, softened
1 (8-ounce) package cream cheese, softened
1½ cups sugar
3 large eggs
1 teaspoon instant coffee granules
1½ teaspoons hot water
¾ cup all-purpose flour
½ cup cocoa
½ cup baking powder
½ teaspoon salt
1½ teaspoons vanilla extract
1 cup chopped pecans

Beat butter and cream cheese at medium speed of an electric mixer until fluffy; gradually add sugar, beating well. Add eggs, one at a time, beating after each addition. Dissolve coffee granules in hot water; add to cream cheese mixture.

Combine flour and next 3 ingredients; add to cream cheese mixture, mixing well. Stir in vanilla and pecans.

Pour batter into a greased 9-inch square pan. Bake at 350° for 30 to 35 minutes. Cool and cut into squares. **Yield: 25 brownies.**

Chocolate Substitution Chart

To substitute for:	Use:
1 (1-ounce) square unsweetened chocolate	• 3 tablespoons cocoa plus 1 tablespoon shortening
1 ounce semisweet chocolate	• 1 ounce (about 3 tablespoons) semisweet chocolate morsels • 1 (1-ounce) square unsweetened chocolate plus 1 tablespoon sugar
4-ounce bar sweet baking chocolate	• ¼ cup cocoa, ⅓ cup sugar, plus 3 tablespoons shortening

White Chocolate Brownies

White Chocolate Brownies

6 (1¼-ounce) white chocolate candy bars with
  almonds, divided
¼ cup butter or margarine
2 large eggs
½ cup sugar
1 cup all-purpose flour
¼ teaspoon baking powder
⅛ teaspoon salt
1 teaspoon vanilla extract
¼ teaspoon almond extract
1 (1-ounce) square semisweet chocolate
1 teaspoon shortening

  Melt 4 candy bars and butter in a heavy
saucepan over low heat, stirring constantly. Set
aside to cool.
  Beat eggs at medium speed of an electric
mixer until thick and pale; gradually add sugar,
beating well.

  Combine flour, baking powder, and salt;
add to egg mixture, mixing well. Stir in cooled
candy mixture and flavorings.
  Coarsely chop remaining 2 candy bars, and
stir into batter. Pour batter into a greased 8-
inch square pan. Bake at 350° for 25 minutes
or until lightly browned. Cool on a wire rack.
  Combine semisweet chocolate and shortening in a small saucepan; cook over low heat,
stirring until chocolate melts. Drizzle over
brownies; chill until chocolate hardens. Cut
into squares. **Yield: 16 brownies.**

Mint Julep Brownies

4 (1-ounce) squares unsweetened chocolate
1 cup butter or margarine
4 large eggs
2 cups sugar
1½ cups all-purpose flour
½ teaspoon salt
2 tablespoons bourbon
1 teaspoon peppermint extract
1 tablespoon powdered sugar
Garnish: fresh mint leaves

  Combine chocolate and butter in a heavy
saucepan; cook over low heat, stirring constantly,
until chocolate melts. Let stand 10 minutes.
  Beat eggs at medium speed of an electric
mixer until thick and pale (about 2 minutes);
gradually add sugar, beating well. Add chocolate
mixture, flour, and next 3 ingredients; beat at low
speed 1 minute.
  Spoon mixture into a lightly greased and
floured 13- x 9- x 2-inch pan. Bake at 350° for
25 to 30 minutes or until a wooden pick inserted
in center comes out clean. Cool on a wire rack
10 minutes. Sprinkle with powdered sugar; cut
into bars. Garnish, if desired. **Yield: 4 dozen.**

Frosted Blonde Brownies

Frosted Blonde Brownies

⅔ cup butter or margarine
1 cup firmly packed brown sugar
1½ cups all-purpose flour
1 teaspoon baking powder
¾ teaspoon ground cinnamon
½ teaspoon salt
2 large eggs
1 cup chopped pecans, lightly toasted
1 tablespoon vanilla extract
1 (6-ounce) package almond brickle chips
    (optional)
Brown Sugar Frosting

Line an 11- x 7- x 1½-inch baking dish with a large sheet of aluminum foil, allowing foil to extend 1 inch out of both ends of dish. Butter foil, and set aside.

Melt ⅔ cup butter and brown sugar in a large skillet over medium heat. Cook until mixture is golden and bubbly (about 5 minutes), stirring frequently. Remove from heat, and transfer to a large mixing bowl.

Combine flour and next 3 ingredients; add to sugar mixture. Beat at medium speed of an electric mixer until blended. Add eggs, beating well.

Stir in pecans, vanilla, and, if desired, brickle chips. Spread batter evenly in foil-lined dish.

Bake at 350° for 25 to 30 minutes. Cool completely. Spread with Brown Sugar Frosting. Let stand at least 30 minutes. Carefully lift foil out of dish. Cut into bars, using a sharp knife. **Yield: 25 brownies.**

Brown Sugar Frosting

¼ cup butter or margarine
1 cup firmly packed brown sugar
¼ cup evaporated milk
1 tablespoon light corn syrup
¼ teaspoon salt
2 teaspoons vanilla extract

Combine first 4 ingredients in a heavy saucepan. Bring to a boil over medium heat; boil 4 minutes. Remove from heat.

Pour into a mixing bowl, and cool completely. Add salt and vanilla; beat at medium-high speed of an electric mixer 3 to 4 minutes or until frosting reaches spreading consistency. Spread over brownies. **Yield: 1 cup.**

Frosted Blonde Brownies Techniques

Line baking dish with a large piece of aluminum foil. This makes it easy to remove baked brownies from dish.

Carefully lift frosted brownies in foil from dish after frosting has set. Remove foil, and cut brownies neatly into bars.

Frosted Peanut Butter Brownies

1 cup butter or margarine
⅓ cup cocoa
2 cups sugar
1½ cups all-purpose flour
½ teaspoon salt
4 large eggs
1 teaspoon vanilla extract
1 (12-ounce) jar chunky peanut butter
½ cup butter or margarine
¼ cup cocoa
⅓ cup milk
10 large marshmallows
1 (16-ounce) package powdered sugar, sifted

Combine 1 cup butter and ⅓ cup cocoa in a saucepan over low heat; cook, stirring frequently, until butter melts. Remove from heat, and cool slightly.

Combine sugar, flour, and salt in a large mixing bowl. Add chocolate mixture, and beat at medium speed of an electric mixer until blended. Add eggs and vanilla, mixing well.

Spread batter in a well-greased 13- x 9- x 2-inch pan. Bake at 350° for 20 to 25 minutes or until a wooden pick inserted in center comes out clean.

Remove lid from peanut butter jar; microwave at MEDIUM (50% power) 2 to 3 minutes or until peanut butter melts, stirring at 1-minute intervals. Spread over warm brownies. Chill about 30 minutes or until set.

Combine ½ cup butter and next 3 ingredients in a saucepan over medium heat; cook, stirring frequently, until marshmallows melt. Remove from heat, and add powdered sugar, stirring until smooth. Spread over peanut butter, and chill until set. Store in refrigerator. **Yield: 4 dozen.**

Note: Freeze brownies in airtight containers up to three months.

Butterscotch Brownies

⅔ cup butter or margarine, softened
1½ cups firmly packed brown sugar
2 large eggs
2 teaspoons vanilla extract
2 cups all-purpose flour
1 teaspoon baking powder
¼ teaspoon baking soda
1 teaspoon salt
1 (6-ounce) package butterscotch morsels
½ cup chopped pecans

Beat butter at medium speed of an electric mixer until creamy; add sugar, beating well. Add eggs and vanilla; beat well.

Combine flour, baking powder, baking soda, and salt; add dry ingredients to creamed mixture, stirring well.

Pour batter into a greased 13- x 9- x 2-inch baking pan. Sprinkle with butterscotch morsels and pecans.

Bake at 350° for 30 minutes. Cool and cut into bars. **Yield: 2½ dozen.**

Blonde Chocolate Chip Brownies

⅓ cup butter or margarine, softened
1 cup firmly packed brown sugar
1 large egg
1 teaspoon vanilla extract
1 cup all-purpose flour
¼ teaspoon baking soda
¼ teaspoon salt
½ cup semisweet chocolate morsels
½ cup chopped pecans

Beat butter at medium speed of an electric mixer until creamy; gradually add brown sugar, beating well. Add egg and vanilla; beat well.

Combine flour, soda, and salt; add to creamed

mixture, and mix well. Stir in chocolate morsels and pecans. Spread mixture in a greased 8-inch square pan.

Bake at 350° for 25 to 30 minutes. Cool and cut into squares. **Yield: 16 brownies.**

Chocolate Chip-Peanut Butter Brownies

⅓ cup butter or margarine, softened
½ cup creamy peanut butter
½ cup sugar
½ cup firmly packed brown sugar
2 large eggs
1 cup all-purpose flour
1 teaspoon baking powder
¼ teaspoon salt
1 teaspoon vanilla extract
1 (6-ounce) package semisweet chocolate
     morsels

Beat butter and peanut butter at medium speed of an electric mixer until creamy; gradually add sugars, beating well. Add eggs, one at a time, beating after each addition.

Combine flour, baking powder, and salt; add to creamed mixture, stirring well. Stir in vanilla and chocolate morsels.

Pour batter into a greased 8-inch square pan. Bake at 350° for 30 to 35 minutes. Cool and cut into squares. **Yield: 25 brownies.**

Almond-Chocolate Bars

1 (8-ounce) package cream cheese, softened
¾ cup butter or margarine, softened
¾ cup sugar
2 cups all-purpose flour
½ teaspoon baking powder
1 teaspoon vanilla extract
1 (6-ounce) package semisweet chocolate
     morsels
½ cup sliced almonds, toasted

Beat cream cheese and butter at medium speed of an electric mixer until fluffy; gradually add sugar, beating well.

Combine flour and baking powder; add to creamed mixture, beating well. Stir in vanilla.

Spread mixture in an ungreased 13- x 9- x 2-inch pan. Bake at 375° for 15 minutes.

Sprinkle chocolate morsels immediately over baked layer; let stand 5 minutes or until chocolate melts. Spread chocolate evenly to edge of pan. Sprinkle with almonds. Cool and cut into bars. **Yield: about 2½ dozen.**

Quick Tip

If you line the pan with aluminum foil when making bar cookies, allow foil to overhang 2 inches on each end. Grease foil if recipe calls for a greased pan. After the cookies have baked and cooled, use the foil overhang to lift the cookie slab from the pan. Cutting the cookies outside the pan keeps the pan from getting scratched and marred.

Almond Cream Squares

Almond Cream Squares

(also pictured on cover)

½ cup butter or margarine
¼ cup sugar
2 tablespoons cocoa
2 teaspoons vanilla extract
¼ teaspoon salt
1 large egg, lightly beaten
1¾ cups vanilla wafer crumbs
1 cup slivered almonds, toasted and chopped
½ cup flaked coconut
Creamy Frosting
2 (1-ounce) squares semisweet chocolate
¼ cup sliced almonds, toasted

Combine first 6 ingredients in a heavy sauce-pan; cook over low heat, stirring constantly, until butter melts and mixture begins to thicken. Remove from heat.

Stir in vanilla wafer crumbs, chopped almonds, and coconut. Press mixture firmly into an ungreased 9-inch square pan. Cover and chill.

Spread Creamy Frosting over chilled almond mixture; cover and chill thoroughly.

Cut chilled mixture into 1½-inch squares. Remove squares from pan; place ½ inch apart on wax paper.

Place chocolate in a small, heavy-duty zip-top plastic bag; seal. Submerge in very hot water until chocolate melts. Snip a tiny hole in one corner of zip-top bag, using scissors.

Pipe chocolate in a decorative design over squares. Top each square with toasted almond slices. **Yield: 3 dozen.**

Creamy Frosting

⅓ cup butter or margarine, softened
3 tablespoons whipping cream
½ teaspoon almond extract
2½ to 3 cups sifted powdered sugar

Beat butter at medium speed of an electric mixer until creamy. Add whipping cream and almond extract; mix well. Gradually add powdered sugar, mixing until frosting is spreading consistency. **Yield: 1½ cups.**

Cream Cheese-Almond Squares

½ cup butter or margarine, softened
2 teaspoons sugar
2 tablespoons milk
½ teaspoon grated lemon rind
1⅓ cups all-purpose flour
2 (8-ounce) packages cream cheese, softened
1 cup sugar
1 large egg, lightly beaten
1 teaspoon grated lemon rind
1 cup chopped almonds, toasted
1 cup sifted powdered sugar
1 tablespoon water
1 teaspoon ground cinnamon
Garnish: toasted sliced almonds

Combine first 4 ingredients; beat at medium speed of an electric mixer until fluffy. Add flour; mix well. Press mixture into a 9-inch square pan; set aside.

Combine cream cheese and next 3 ingredients; beat until smooth. Stir in chopped almonds; pour mixture over layer in pan. Bake at 300° for 1 hour and 10 minutes or until set.

Combine powdered sugar, water, and cinnamon; mix well. Spread over hot mixture; cool. Chill 3 to 4 hours; cut into squares. Garnish, if desired. **Yield: 3 dozen.**

Yummy Bars

Yummy Bars

1 (14-ounce) package caramels, unwrapped
1 (5-ounce) can evaporated milk, divided
1 (18.25-ounce) package German chocolate
    cake mix with pudding
¾ cup butter or margarine, melted
1 large egg
1 (6-ounce) package semisweet chocolate
    morsels
1 cup coarsely chopped pecans

Combine caramels and ¼ cup evaporated milk in a small, heavy saucepan. Cook over low heat, stirring occasionally, until smooth; set aside.

Combine cake mix, butter, egg, and remaining evaporated milk. Spoon half of mixture into a greased 13- x 9- x 2-inch pan, spreading mixture evenly.

Bake at 350° for 6 minutes. Remove from oven; sprinkle with morsels and pecans. Spoon caramel mixture on top; carefully spoon remaining cake mixture over caramel layer.

Bake at 350° for 20 to 25 minutes. Cool on a wire rack, and cut into bars. **Yield: about 3 dozen.**

German Chocolate Chess Squares

1 (18.25-ounce) package German chocolate
    cake mix with pudding
1 large egg, lightly beaten
½ cup butter or margarine, melted
1 cup chopped pecans
1 (8-ounce) package cream cheese, softened
2 large eggs
1 (16-ounce) package powdered sugar, sifted

Combine first 4 ingredients in a large bowl, stirring until dry ingredients are moistened. Press into a greased 13- x 9- x 2-inch pan; set aside.

Combine cream cheese, 2 eggs, and 1 cup powdered sugar; beat at medium speed of an electric mixer until blended. Gradually add remaining powdered sugar, beating after each addition. Pour over chocolate layer, spreading evenly.

Bake at 350° for 40 minutes. Cool on a wire rack, and cut into squares. **Yield: 4 dozen.**

Choco-Crumble Squares

1½ cups all-purpose flour
¾ cup firmly packed brown sugar
¼ teaspoon salt
½ cup butter or margarine, softened
1 (6-ounce) package semisweet chocolate
    morsels
1 cup creamy peanut butter

Combine first 3 ingredients; cut in butter with a pastry blender until mixture is crumbly. Pat mixture into an ungreased 13- x 9- x 2-inch pan. Bake at 375° for 10 minutes.

Combine chocolate morsels and peanut butter in a small saucepan; cook over low heat, stirring constantly, until chocolate melts. Spread over crust; chill until firm. Cut into squares. Store in refrigerator, and serve chilled. **Yield: 3 dozen.**

Melting Chocolate

• Save on cleanup by melting 1-ounce, paper-wrapped squares of chocolate in the microwave. Keep chocolate in the paper, and microwave at MEDIUM (50% power); 1 square takes 1½ to 2 minutes, 2 squares about 3 minutes, and 3 squares about 4 minutes.

• Semisweet chocolate morsels and squares hold their shape when melted until they are stirred.

Butter Pecan Turtle Bars

½ cup butter or margarine, softened
1 cup firmly packed brown sugar
2 cups all-purpose flour
1 cup chopped pecans
⅔ cup butter or margarine, melted
½ cup firmly packed brown sugar
1 cup milk chocolate morsels

Beat ½ cup butter at medium speed of an electric mixer until creamy; add 1 cup brown sugar, beating well. Gradually add flour, mixing well. Press mixture into an ungreased 13- x 9- x 2-inch pan. Sprinkle with pecans; set aside.

Combine ⅔ cup butter and ½ cup brown sugar in a small saucepan. Bring to a boil over medium heat, stirring constantly. Boil 30 seconds, stirring constantly. Remove from heat, and pour hot mixture over crust.

Bake at 350° for 18 minutes or until bubbly. Remove from oven; immediately sprinkle with chocolate morsels. Let stand 2 to 3 minutes; cut through chocolate with a knife to create a marble effect. Cool. Cut into bars. **Yield: 4 dozen.**

By-Cracky Bars

¾ cup shortening
1 cup sugar
2 large eggs
1¾ cups all-purpose flour
¼ teaspoon baking soda
1 teaspoon salt
⅓ cup milk
1 teaspoon vanilla extract
1 (1-ounce) square unsweetened chocolate, melted
¾ cup chopped walnuts
8 or 9 double graham crackers
1 (6-ounce) package semisweet chocolate morsels

Beat shortening at medium speed of an electric mixer until fluffy; add sugar, beating well. Add eggs, beating well.

Combine flour, soda, and salt; add to creamed mixture alternately with milk, mixing after each addition. Stir in vanilla.

Place one-third of batter in another bowl, and add unsweetened chocolate and walnuts to this mixture. Spread chocolate mixture in a greased 13- x 9- x 2-inch pan. Arrange 8 or 9 double graham crackers over batter.

Add chocolate morsels to remaining two-thirds batter, and drop by spoonfuls over graham crackers. Spread batter to cover. Bake at 375° for 25 minutes. Cool and cut into bars. **Yield: 3 dozen.**

Chocolate Chip Squares

2 (20-ounce) rolls refrigerated chocolate chip cookie dough
2 (8-ounce) packages cream cheese, softened
1½ cups sugar
2 large eggs

Freeze rolls of cookie dough; slice one roll of frozen cookie dough into 40 (⅛-inch) slices. Arrange cookie slices in a well-greased 15- x 10- x 1-inch jellyroll pan. Press cookie dough together to form bottom crust. Set aside.

Beat cream cheese at high speed of an electric mixer until fluffy; gradually add sugar, and mix well. Add eggs, one at a time, beating after each addition. Pour cream cheese mixture over cookie dough layer in pan.

Slice remaining frozen roll of cookie dough into 40 (⅛-inch) slices, and arrange over cream cheese mixture.

Bake at 350° for 45 minutes. Cool and cut into squares. **Yield: 4 dozen.**

Chocolate Chip Squares

Lemon Hearts

Lemon Hearts

2 cups all-purpose flour
½ cup sifted powdered sugar
1 cup butter or margarine, softened
1 teaspoon vanilla extract
2 cups sugar
2 tablespoons cornstarch
5 large eggs, beaten
1 tablespoon grated lemon rind
¼ cup plus 2 tablespoons lemon juice
2 tablespoons butter or margarine, melted
2 to 4 tablespoons powdered sugar
Garnish: lemon rind knots

Combine first 4 ingredients; beat at low speed of an electric mixer until blended. Pat mixture into a greased 13- x 9- x 2-inch baking dish. Bake at 350° for 18 minutes or until golden.

Combine 2 cups sugar and cornstarch. Add eggs and next 3 ingredients; beat well. Pour mixture over crust.

Bake at 350° for 20 to 25 minutes or until set. Cool and chill well. Sift powdered sugar over top, and cut into hearts or squares. Garnish, if desired. **Yield: 14 hearts or 2½ dozen squares.**

Nutty Apricot Bars

2 (6-ounce) packages dried apricots
¾ cup sugar
¾ cup butter or margarine, softened
1 cup sugar
2 cups all-purpose flour
½ teaspoon baking soda
¼ teaspoon salt
1 (3-ounce) can flaked coconut
½ cup chopped pecans or walnuts

Cover apricots with water, and bring to a boil; reduce heat, and simmer, uncovered, 15 minutes or until tender. Drain, reserving ¼ cup liquid.

Coarsely chop apricots, and set aside.

Combine reserved apricot liquid and ¾ cup sugar in a saucepan; simmer 5 minutes. Stir in chopped apricots.

Beat butter at medium speed of an electric mixer until creamy. Add 1 cup sugar; beat well.

Combine flour, soda, and salt; add to creamed mixture, mixing well (mixture will be crumbly). Stir in coconut and pecans.

Pat about three-fourths of coconut mixture into an ungreased 13- x 9- x 2-inch pan. Bake at 350° for 10 minutes.

Spread apricot mixture evenly over crust, spreading to within ¼ inch from edge of pan. Sprinkle with remaining coconut mixture. Bake 30 additional minutes.

Cool in pan; chill. Cut into bars. Store in refrigerator. **Yield: about 4 dozen.**

Date Squares

1½ cups regular oats, uncooked
1½ cups all-purpose flour
¼ teaspoon baking soda
¼ teaspoon salt
1 cup firmly packed brown sugar
¾ cup shortening
2 (8-ounce) packages whole pitted dates
1 cup water
½ cup sugar

Combine first 5 ingredients in a bowl; cut in shortening with a pastry blender until crumbly. Reserve 1 cup crumb mixture; press remaining mixture into an ungreased 13- x 9- x 2-inch pan.

Chop dates. Combine dates, water, and sugar in a saucepan. Bring to a boil; reduce heat, and simmer 1 minute, stirring constantly. Spread date mixture over crumb mixture. Sprinkle with reserved 1 cup crumb mixture.

Bake at 350° for 25 to 30 minutes. Cool and cut into squares. **Yield: 4 dozen.**

Golden Bars

1½ cups all-purpose flour
½ cup firmly packed brown sugar
½ cup butter or margarine, softened
2 large eggs, beaten
1 cup firmly packed brown sugar
2 tablespoons all-purpose flour
½ teaspoon baking powder
¼ teaspoon salt
½ teaspoon vanilla extract
1¼ cups flaked coconut
½ cup chopped pecans

Combine flour and ½ cup brown sugar; cut in butter with a pastry blender until mixture is crumbly. Press mixture into a lightly greased 9-inch square pan. Bake at 350° for 15 minutes.

Combine eggs and next 5 ingredients, mixing well. Stir in coconut and pecans. Pour egg mixture over crust.

Bake at 350° for 20 minutes. Cool and cut into bars. **Yield: 3 dozen.**

Praline Grahams

Praline Grahams

1 (5⅓-ounce) package graham crackers
¾ cup butter or margarine
½ cup sugar
1 cup chopped pecans

Separate each graham cracker into four sections. Arrange in an ungreased 15- x 10- x 1-inch jellyroll pan with edges touching.

Melt butter in a saucepan; stir in sugar and pecans. Bring to a boil; cook 3 minutes, stirring frequently. Spread mixture evenly over graham crackers.

Bake at 300° for 12 minutes. Remove from pan, and cool on wax paper. **Yield: 3½ dozen.**

Pecan Bars

1¾ cups all-purpose flour
⅓ cup firmly packed brown sugar
¾ cup butter or margarine
1 cup firmly packed brown sugar
4 large eggs
1 cup dark corn syrup
¼ cup butter or margarine, melted
⅛ teaspoon salt
1¼ cups chopped pecans

Combine flour and ⅓ cup brown sugar. Cut in ¾ cup butter with a pastry blender until mixture is crumbly. Press mixture evenly into a greased 13- x 9- x 2-inch pan. Bake at 350° for 15 to 17 minutes.

Combine 1 cup brown sugar, eggs, and next 3

ingredients, beating well. Stir in pecans. Pour filling over prepared crust.

Bake at 350° for 35 to 40 minutes or until firm. Cool and cut into bars. **Yield: about 2½ dozen.**

Jam-it Bars

2 cups all-purpose flour
¼ teaspoon salt
½ cup sugar
½ teaspoon vanilla extract
⅛ teaspoon ground cinnamon
⅛ teaspoon ground nutmeg
¾ cup butter or margarine
1 cup chopped pecans, divided
1 (10-ounce) jar peach jam or preserves

Combine first 6 ingredients; cut in butter with a pastry blender until mixture is crumbly. Stir in ½ cup pecans. Remove ¾ cup of mixture, and set aside.

Press remaining mixture evenly into a lightly greased 9-inch square pan. Spread peach jam over crumb mixture; sprinkle with remaining ½ cup pecans. Sprinkle reserved crumb mixture over pecans.

Bake at 350° for 35 to 40 minutes; cool. Cut into bars. **Yield: about 2 dozen.**

Granola Bars

4 cups regular oats, uncooked
⅔ cup butter or margarine, melted
½ cup firmly packed brown sugar
⅓ cup honey
1 large egg, lightly beaten
½ teaspoon salt
½ teaspoon vanilla extract
1 cup chopped pecans
1 cup raisins

Place oats in an ungreased 15- x 10- x 1-inch jellyroll pan. Bake at 350° for 15 minutes, stirring at 5-minute intervals; set aside.

Combine butter and remaining ingredients; add oats, and mix well. Spread mixture evenly into lightly greased jellyroll pan.

Bake at 350° for 25 minutes. Cool completely, and cut into bars. **Yield: 5 dozen.**

Peanut Butter Bars

1 (6-ounce) package semisweet chocolate
     morsels
½ cup butter or margarine, softened
⅔ cup creamy peanut butter
1 cup firmly packed brown sugar
1 large egg
1 teaspoon vanilla extract
1¼ cups all-purpose flour
½ teaspoon baking soda
½ teaspoon salt
1½ cups quick-cooking oats, uncooked

Melt chocolate in a heavy saucepan over low heat; set aside.

Beat butter and peanut butter at medium speed of an electric mixer until creamy. Add sugar, egg, and vanilla, mixing well.

Combine flour, soda, and salt; stir into creamed mixture. Stir in oats.

Press three-fourths of peanut butter mixture into a greased 13- x 9- x 2-inch pan. Spread chocolate over top. Crumble remaining peanut butter mixture over chocolate.

Bake at 350° for 18 to 20 minutes. Cool and cut into bars. **Yield: 2 dozen.**

Pizza Cookie

¾ **cup butter or margarine, softened**
1 **cup sugar**
1 **large egg**
1½ **cups all-purpose flour**
½ **teaspoon baking soda**
¼ **teaspoon salt**
¼ **cup cocoa**
1 **teaspoon vanilla extract**
¾ **cup candy-coated chocolate pieces, divided**
½ **cup chopped pecans, divided**
¼ **cup flaked coconut**
½ **cup miniature marshmallows**

Line a 12-inch pizza pan with heavy-duty aluminum foil; grease foil, and set aside.

Beat butter at medium speed of an electric mixer until creamy; gradually add sugar, beating well. Add egg, and beat well.

Combine flour and next 3 ingredients; add to creamed mixture, mixing well. Add vanilla, and mix well. Stir in ½ cup chocolate pieces and ¼ cup chopped pecans.

Spoon batter onto prepared pan, spreading to within 1 inch of edge. Sprinkle with coconut and remaining ¼ cup pecans.

Bake at 350° for 15 minutes. Sprinkle marshmallows and remaining ¼ cup chocolate pieces on top; bake 5 to 7 minutes. Cool on a wire rack. **Yield: one 12-inch cookie.**

Christmas Fruit Squares

½ **cup butter, softened**
1½ **cups firmly packed brown sugar**
2 **large eggs**
1 **cup self-rising flour, divided**
2 **cups chopped pecans**
½ **pound red or green candied cherries, chopped**
½ **pound yellow candied pineapple, chopped**
½ **cup flaked coconut**

Beat butter at medium speed of an electric mixer until creamy; gradually add sugar, beating well. Add eggs, one at a time, beating after each addition. Add ¾ cup flour; stir well.

Combine pecans and remaining ingredients; dredge in ¼ cup flour. Stir fruit mixture into batter. Spoon into a greased and floured 9-inch square pan.

Bake at 300° for 1 hour and 10 minutes or until a wooden pick inserted in center comes out clean. Cool in pan on a wire rack. Chill before cutting. **Yield: 3 dozen.**

Zucchini Bars

1½ **cups firmly packed brown sugar**
½ **cup butter or margarine, softened**
¼ **cup vegetable oil**
2 **large eggs**
2 **tablespoons water**
1 **teaspoon vanilla extract**
¼ **teaspoon ground nutmeg**
1½ **cups shreds of wheat bran cereal**
1½ **cups all-purpose flour**
½ **cup whole wheat flour**
1 **teaspoon baking soda**
½ **teaspoon salt**
2½ **cups grated zucchini**
1 **cup raisins**
1 **cup flaked coconut**

Combine first 3 ingredients in a large mixing bowl; beat at medium speed of an electric mixer until fluffy. Add eggs and next 3 ingredients; mix just until blended.

Combine cereal and next 4 ingredients; add to creamed mixture alternately with zucchini, beginning and ending with flour mixture. Mix just until blended. Stir in raisins and coconut.

Spoon batter into a greased 13- x 9- x 2-inch pan. Bake at 350° for 40 minutes. Cool and cut into bars. **Yield: 3 dozen.**

Holiday Treasure Chest

Spiced by tradition, baked by the dozens, and decorated with love,
Christmas cookies are always a welcome treat. Whether baked for
family or friends, these cookies have their own special magic.

Favorite Chocolate Chip Cookies, Caramel-Filled Chocolate Cookies

Shortbread Cookies, Double-Chocolate Cheesecake Squares, Cocoa Surprise Cookies

Easy Peanut Butter Cookies, Lemon Crinkle Cookies, Brandied Fruitcake Cookies

Snow Flurries, Ribbon Cookies, Christmas Tree Sandwich Cookies

Braided Candy Canes, Cherry Crowns, and Sugar-Coated
Chocolate Cookies (page 132)

Favorite Chocolate Chip Cookies

2½ cups quick-cooking oats, uncooked
2¼ cups all-purpose flour
1 teaspoon baking powder
1 teaspoon baking soda
1 teaspoon salt
1 cup butter or margarine, softened
1 cup sugar
1 cup firmly packed brown sugar
2 large eggs, lightly beaten
¾ teaspoon vanilla extract
¾ teaspoon dark rum (optional)
1 (6-ounce) package semisweet chocolate morsels
1 (6-ounce) package milk chocolate morsels
2 ounces white chocolate baking bar, cut into pieces
1 cup chopped pecans

Place oats in container of an electric blender; process 30 seconds or until oats turn to powder. Combine oat powder, flour, and next 3 ingredients. Set aside.

Beat butter at medium speed of an electric mixer until creamy; gradually add sugars, beating well. Add eggs, vanilla, and rum, if desired, beating well. Gradually stir in flour mixture. Stir in chocolate morsels and remaining ingredients. Cover and chill 2 hours.

Shape dough into 1-inch balls; place 3 inches apart on ungreased cookie sheets. Bake at 350° for 10 to 12 minutes. (For chewy texture, do not overbake.) **Yield: 4 dozen.**

Caramel-Filled Chocolate Cookies

1 cup butter or margarine, softened
1 cup sugar
1 cup firmly packed brown sugar
2 large eggs
2¼ cups all-purpose flour
¾ cup cocoa
1 teaspoon baking soda
2 teaspoons vanilla extract
1 cup chopped pecans, divided
1 tablespoon sugar
1 (9-ounce) package chewy caramels in milk chocolate

Beat butter at medium speed of an electric mixer until creamy; gradually add sugars, beating well. Add eggs; beat well.

Combine flour, cocoa, and soda; add to creamed mixture, mixing well. Stir in vanilla and ½ cup pecans. Cover and chill 8 hours.

Combine remaining ½ cup pecans and 1 tablespoon sugar; set aside.

Divide dough into 4 equal portions. Work with one portion of dough at a time, storing remainder in refrigerator. Divide each portion into 12 equal pieces.

Gently press each piece of cookie dough around each candy, forming a ball; dip one side of ball in pecan mixture. Place balls, pecan side up, 2 inches apart on ungreased cookie sheets.

Bake at 375° for 8 minutes. (Cookies will look soft.) Let cool 1 minute on cookie sheets. Remove to wire racks to cool. **Yield: 4 dozen.**

Kids in the Kitchen

Turn your kitchen into a children's workshop and make cookies for Santa or gift giving. The two simple recipes on page 111 are perfect choices—they have few ingredients and only a few steps. And for a bonus, they combine two favorites—chocolate and peanut butter!

Chocolate-Peanut Butter Cups

1 (20-ounce) package refrigerated sliceable
   peanut butter cookie dough
48 miniature peanut butter cup candies,
   unwrapped

Cut cookie dough into ¾-inch slices; cut each slice into quarters. Place quarters in greased miniature (1¾-inch) muffin pans (do not shape).

Bake at 350° for 9 minutes (dough will puff during baking). Remove from oven, and immediately press a peanut butter cup candy gently into each cookie cup. Cool completely before removing from pans. Chill until firm. **Yield: 4 dozen.**

Easy Peanut Butter Cookies

1 large egg, lightly beaten
1 cup chunky peanut butter
1 cup sugar
36 milk chocolate kisses, unwrapped

Combine first 3 ingredients; shape into ¾-inch balls. Place on ungreased cookie sheets.

Bake at 350° for 10 minutes. Immediately press a chocolate kiss in center of each cookie; remove to wire racks to cool. **Yield: 3 dozen.**

Easy Peanut Butter Cookies

Fruitcake Cookies

2 cups chopped pecans
½ pound yellow candied pineapple, chopped
½ pound red and green candied cherries, chopped
½ pound golden raisins
¼ cup all-purpose flour
½ cup butter or margarine, softened
1 cup firmly packed brown sugar
4 large eggs
2½ cups all-purpose flour
1 teaspoon baking soda
¾ teaspoon ground cardamom

Combine first 5 ingredients in a large bowl, tossing to coat fruit and nuts with flour. Set aside.

Beat butter at medium speed of an electric mixer until creamy; gradually add brown sugar, beating well. Add eggs; beat well.

Combine 2½ cups flour, soda, and cardamom; gradually add to creamed mixture, beating well. Stir in fruit mixture.

Drop dough by heaping teaspoonfuls 2 inches apart onto lightly greased cookie sheets.

Bake at 350° for 12 minutes or until lightly browned. Cool slightly on cookie sheets; remove to wire racks to cool completely. **Yield: 9½ dozen.**

Brandied Fruitcake Cookies

2 (8-ounce) packages yellow candied pineapple, chopped
1 (8-ounce) package red candied cherries, chopped
1 (8-ounce) package green candied cherries, chopped
2 cups golden raisins
4 cups chopped pecans or walnuts
3½ cups all-purpose flour, divided
½ cup butter or margarine, softened
1 cup firmly packed brown sugar
4 large eggs, separated
1 tablespoon baking soda
3 tablespoons milk
¼ cup brandy
1 teaspoon ground cinnamon
1 teaspoon ground nutmeg

Combine first 5 ingredients; dredge with 1 cup flour, stirring well. Set aside.

Beat butter at medium speed of an electric mixer until creamy; gradually add sugar, beating well. Add egg yolks, mixing well.

Dissolve soda in milk; add to creamed mixture. Add brandy, spices, and remaining 2½ cups flour, mixing well.

Beat egg whites until stiff; fold into batter. Fold in fruit mixture.

Drop dough by rounded teaspoonfuls onto greased cookie sheets. Bake at 325° for 12 to 15 minutes. Cool on wire racks. **Yield: about 10 dozen.**

Packing Cookies to Mail

• Bar and drop cookies tend to travel well. Select ones high in sugar and shortening that won't dry out or crumble during the journey.
• Fragile or brittle cookies, such as sugar cookies, are apt to crumble when mailed. Avoid mailing cookies with frostings or moist fillings as they may become sticky.
• Wrap crisp and soft cookies separately to preserve their texture. Wrap cookies in pairs, back to back, or in small stacks with plastic wrap or aluminum foil.

Thumbprint Cookies

1 cup butter or margarine, softened
⅔ cup sugar
2 egg yolks
½ teaspoon vanilla extract
2¼ cups all-purpose flour
¼ teaspoon salt
Chocolate Frosting or Powdered Sugar Glaze

Beat butter at medium speed of an electric mixer until creamy; gradually add sugar, beating well. Add egg yolks, one at a time, beating after each addition. Stir in vanilla.

Combine flour and salt; add to creamed mixture, mixing well. Chill dough at least 1 hour.

Shape dough into 1-inch balls; place about 2 inches apart on ungreased cookie sheets. Press thumb in each cookie, leaving an indentation.

Bake at 300° for 20 to 25 minutes; do not brown. Cool on wire racks. Spoon about ½ teaspoon Chocolate Frosting or Powdered Sugar Glaze in each cookie indentation. **Yield: 3½ dozen.**

Chocolate Frosting

1 cup sugar
¼ cup cocoa
¼ cup milk
¼ cup butter or margarine
½ teaspoon vanilla extract

Combine first 3 ingredients in a saucepan. Bring to a boil; boil 1½ to 2 minutes, stirring constantly. Remove from heat; stir in butter and vanilla. Beat until mixture cools slightly. **Yield: 1 cup.**

Powdered Sugar Glaze

2 cups sifted powdered sugar
3 to 4 tablespoons milk
½ teaspoon vanilla extract
Few drops of desired food coloring

Combine powdered sugar, milk, vanilla extract, and food coloring, stirring until smooth. **Yield: 1 cup.**

Note: One cup strawberry preserves may be substituted for frosting or glaze. If so, bake cookies 15 minutes. Spoon preserves into indentations, and bake 5 additional minutes.

Apricot Kolaches

1 cup butter or margarine, softened
2 (3-ounce) packages cream cheese, softened
2 tablespoons sugar
2 cups all-purpose flour
Apricot Filling
Powdered sugar (optional)

Beat butter and cream cheese at medium speed of an electric mixer until creamy; add sugar, beating well. Add flour, and mix well. Shape dough into a ball; cover and chill 1 hour.

Work with half of dough at a time. Turn dough out onto a well-floured surface. Roll dough to ⅛-inch thickness; cut into 2-inch squares. Spoon about ½ teaspoon Apricot Filling in center of each square. Bring corners of square to center, pinching edges to seal.

Place cookies on ungreased cookie sheets. Bake at 400° for 15 minutes. Cool on wire racks. Sprinkle with powdered sugar, if desired. **Yield: about 7 dozen.**

Apricot Filling

¾ cup dried apricots
1½ cups water
¾ cup sugar

Combine apricots and water in a heavy saucepan; cover and cook over medium heat about 10 minutes or until apricots are soft. Cook, uncovered, 5 minutes or until most of water has been absorbed. Remove from heat. Mash apricots, and stir in sugar. **Yield: 1 cup.**

Snow Flurries

Snow Flurries

½ **cup butter or margarine, softened**
½ **cup shortening**
1 **cup sugar**
2 **large eggs**
1 **tablespoon grated lemon rind**
1 **teaspoon vanilla extract**
½ **teaspoon almond extract**
3½ **cups all-purpose flour**
½ **teaspoon baking powder**
½ **teaspoon salt**
⅓ **cup raspberry jam**
1 **cup sifted powdered sugar**

Beat butter and shortening at medium speed of an electric mixer until fluffy; gradually add 1 cup sugar, beating well. Add eggs, lemon rind, and flavorings, mixing well.

Combine flour, baking powder, and salt; gradually add to creamed mixture, mixing well. Cover and chill 1 hour.

Divide dough into 2 equal portions; store 1 portion in refrigerator. Roll remaining portion to ⅛-inch thickness on a lightly floured surface. Cut with a 2½-inch star-shaped cookie cutter, and place on ungreased cookie sheets.

Bake at 375° for 7 to 8 minutes or until lightly browned; cool 2 minutes on cookie sheets. Remove to wire racks to cool. Repeat with remaining dough.

Spread center of half of cookies with about ¼ teaspoon raspberry jam just before serving. Place a second cookie on top, alternating points of stars of top and bottom cookies. Sprinkle generously with powdered sugar. **Yield: 5 dozen.**

Apricot Wonders

1½ cups shortening
1½ cups sugar
2 large eggs
1 tablespoon grated orange rind
1 teaspoon vanilla extract
4 cups all-purpose flour
1 tablespoon baking powder
½ teaspoon salt
2 to 3 tablespoons milk
Apricot Filling

Beat shortening at medium speed of an electric mixer until fluffy; gradually add sugar, beating well. Add eggs, one at a time, beating after each addition. Stir in orange rind and vanilla.

Combine flour, baking powder, and salt; add to creamed mixture alternately with milk, mixing after each addition. Cover and chill.

Roll dough to ⅛-inch thickness on a lightly floured surface. Cut with a 3-inch star-shaped cookie cutter, and place on lightly greased cookie sheets. Use a ½-inch star-shaped cutter to cut out a star in half of cookies.

Bake at 350° for 8 minutes. Remove to wire racks to cool. Spread each solid cookie with about 1 teaspoon Apricot Filling, and top with a cutout cookie. **Yield: 4½ dozen.**

Apricot Filling

1 (6-ounce) package dried apricots
½ cup sugar
½ cup water

Combine all ingredients in a small saucepan; bring to a boil over medium heat. Reduce heat, and simmer about 15 minutes or until tender. Spoon into container of an electric blender or food processor; process until smooth. **Yield: 1 cup.**

Note: Cookies and Apricot Filling may be frozen separately up to six months. To serve, thaw cookies and filling, and assemble as directed.

Date-Filled Cookies

(pictured on page 116)

1 cup shortening
½ cup sugar
½ cup firmly packed brown sugar
1 large egg
3 tablespoons milk
1 teaspoon vanilla extract
3 cups all-purpose flour
½ teaspoon baking soda
½ teaspoon salt
1 cup chopped dates
¼ cup sugar
Pinch of salt
¼ cup water
1 tablespoon lemon juice

Beat shortening at medium speed of an electric mixer until fluffy; gradually add ½ cup each of sugar and brown sugar, beating well. Add egg, milk, and vanilla, mixing well.

Combine flour, soda, and salt; gradually add dry ingredients to creamed mixture, mixing well.

Use a cookie press to shape dough into 2-inch flowers. (Using a small paring knife, lift center circle from half of flowers.)

Bake at 375° for 10 to 12 minutes. Remove to wire racks to cool completely.

Combine dates and next 3 ingredients; bring to a boil. Cover, reduce heat, and simmer 5 minutes, stirring occasionally. Add lemon juice. Cool.

Turn half of cookies bottom up, and spread each with 1 teaspoon filling just before serving. Place a second cookie, with center part removed, on top of filling (top side up). **Yield: 3 dozen.**

Filled Meringue Trees, Christmas Mints, and Date-Filled Cookies (page 115)

Filled Meringue Trees

2¼ cups sifted powdered sugar
3 egg whites
Green paste food coloring
Chocolate Buttercream

Line two large cookie sheets with unglazed brown paper. Sketch 24 (3½-inch-long) Christmas trees onto paper. Set aside.

Combine powdered sugar and egg whites in top of a double boiler. Beat at low speed of an electric mixer 30 seconds or just until blended.

Place over boiling water; beat constantly on high speed 5 to 7 minutes or until stiff peaks form. Remove from heat.

Fit tip No. 22 into decorating bag. Using a small art brush, paint about a ¼-inch-wide stripe of food coloring inside bag from tip end to outer edge.

Spoon meringue mixture into bag; close bag securely. Starting at top of tree and using a zigzag motion, pipe trees.

Bake at 300° for 25 minutes. Remove from oven; cool on cookie sheets. Carefully peel away paper. Store in an airtight container at room temperature up to 2 days.

Pipe or spread Chocolate Buttercream on flat sides of half of meringue trees, before serving; top with remaining trees. **Yield: 1 dozen.**

Chocolate Buttercream

⅓ cup butter or margarine, softened
¾ cup plus 2 tablespoons sifted powdered sugar
1½ tablespoons cocoa
½ teaspoon vanilla extract
1 to 2 teaspoons milk

Beat butter at medium speed of an electric mixer until creamy; gradually add sugar, beating well. Add cocoa, vanilla, and enough milk to make a good spreading consistency; beat well. **Yield: about ⅔ cup.**

Christmas Mints

½ cup butter or margarine, softened
1 (16-ounce) package powdered sugar, sifted
2 tablespoons milk
2 tablespoons finely crushed hard peppermint candy
⅛ teaspoon oil of peppermint
About 20 (2-ounce) squares chocolate flavored candy coating
Decorator Frosting

Beat butter at medium speed of electric mixer until creamy; gradually add sugar, beating well. Stir in milk and next 2 ingredients, mixing well.

Divide mixture into 4 portions; shape each into a ball. Roll out each portion to ¼-inch thickness; cut with a 1-inch round cutter. Place on cookie sheets; cover and chill.

Melt candy coating in a large heavy saucepan over low heat, stirring often. Dip chilled mints in coating to cover all sides, allowing excess to drip. Place on wax paper-lined cookie sheets. Chill mints until coating hardens.

Pipe green Decorator Frosting on mints, using tip No. 65, to make holly leaves, and pipe red frosting, using tip No. 2, to make holly berries. (No. 2 can also be used to make trees, stockings, wreaths, and candles.) **Yield: 8 dozen.**

Decorator Frosting

3 tablespoons butter or margarine, softened
2 cups sifted powdered sugar
2 tablespoons milk
½ teaspoon vanilla extract
Red and green paste food coloring

Beat butter and sugar at medium speed of an electric mixer until fluffy. Add milk and vanilla, beating to spreading consistency. Divide into thirds; color one-third of frosting red and remaining two-thirds green. **Yield: 1¼ cups.**

Lemon Crinkle Cookies

½ cup shortening
1 cup firmly packed brown sugar
1 large egg
1 tablespoon grated lemon rind
1½ cups all-purpose flour
½ teaspoon baking soda
Pinch of salt
½ teaspoon cream of tartar
¼ teaspoon ground ginger
2 tablespoons sugar

Beat shortening at medium speed of an electric mixer until fluffy; gradually add brown sugar, beating well. Add egg and lemon rind, beating well.

Combine flour and next 4 ingredients; gradually add to creamed mixture, beating just until blended. Cover and chill 15 minutes.

Shape dough into 1-inch balls. Roll balls in 2 tablespoons sugar; place 2 inches apart on ungreased cookie sheets.

Bake at 350° for 12 minutes or until lightly browned. Cool slightly on cookie sheets; remove to wire racks to cool completely. **Yield: 3 dozen.**

Bourbon Balls

2 cups vanilla wafer crumbs
2 cups chopped pecans or walnuts
2 cups sifted powdered sugar
¼ cup cocoa
¼ cup light corn syrup
¼ cup plus 2 tablespoons bourbon
Sifted powdered sugar

Combine first 4 ingredients, and stir well. Combine corn syrup and bourbon; stir into crumb mixture, and shape into 1-inch balls.

Roll each ball in powdered sugar. Store in an airtight container. **Yield: about 4 dozen.**

Peppermint Patties

(also pictured on cover)

1 cup butter or margarine, softened
1½ cups sugar
1 large egg
1 to 1½ teaspoons peppermint extract
2½ cups all-purpose flour
1½ teaspoons baking powder
¼ teaspoon salt
Red paste food coloring

Beat butter at medium speed of an electric mixer until creamy; gradually add sugar, beating well. Add egg and peppermint extract; beat well.

Combine flour, baking powder, and salt; add to creamed mixture, beating just until blended.

Divide dough in half; add a few drops of red food coloring to one half, and knead until color is distributed. Cover and chill both halves until firm.

Divide each half of dough into 2 equal portions. Roll out each portion on floured wax paper into an 8-inch square, trimming edges if necessary. Invert one white dough square onto one red dough square; peel wax paper from white dough.

Tightly roll dough jellyroll fashion, peeling wax paper from red dough as you roll. Repeat with remaining dough. Cover and chill at least 2 hours.

Cut roll of dough into ¼-inch slices; place on ungreased cookie sheets. Bake at 350° for 10 minutes. Transfer to wire racks to cool. **Yield: about 5 dozen.**

Quick Tip

To give a pretty shine to plain sugar cookies, beat an egg white until frothy and brush over unbaked cookies. Sprinkle with sugar and bake.

Gingerbread Men

2¼ cups sugar
¾ cup water
⅓ cup dark corn syrup
1 tablespoon ground cinnamon
1 tablespoon ground ginger
2 teaspoons ground cloves
1 cup butter or margarine
1 tablespoon baking soda
1 tablespoon water
8 cups all-purpose flour
Raisins

Combine first 6 ingredients in a medium saucepan; cook over medium heat, stirring until sugar dissolves. Add butter, stirring until melted.

Dissolve soda in 1 tablespoon water; add to sugar mixture. Pour sugar mixture into a large bowl; gradually add flour, mixing well. Cover and chill at least 2 hours.

Divide dough into thirds. Roll one-third of dough to ¼- to ⅛-inch thickness on a lightly floured surface. Cut with a 4-inch gingerbread man cutter, and place on a lightly greased cookie sheet; place raisins on Gingerbread Men as desired.

Bake at 350° for 10 to 12 minutes. Cool 1 minute on cookie sheet; remove to wire racks, and cool completely. Repeat procedure with remaining dough. **Yield: about 3½ dozen.**

Note: Cookie molds may be used in place of cookie cutters. Baking times will vary with size of mold.

From left: Gingerbread Men, Bourbon Balls, and Peppermint Patties

Gingerbread Animal Cookies

Gingerbread Animal Cookies

½ cup shortening
½ cup sugar
½ cup molasses
¼ cup water
2½ cups all-purpose flour
½ teaspoon baking soda
¾ teaspoon salt
¾ teaspoon ground ginger
¼ teaspoon ground nutmeg
Tubes of decorator frosting (optional)

Beat shortening at medium speed of an electric mixer until fluffy; gradually add sugar, beating well. Add molasses and water; beat well.

Combine flour and next 4 ingredients; add to creamed mixture, mixing well. Cover and chill dough several hours.

Work with one-fourth of dough at a time; store remainder in refrigerator. Roll dough to ¼-inch thickness on an ungreased cookie sheet. Cut with assorted 2- to 3-inch cookie cutters; remove excess dough.

Bake at 375° for 6 to 8 minutes. Cool 2 minutes. Transfer to wire racks to cool. Repeat procedure with remaining dough. Decorate with colored frosting, if desired. **Yield: about 4 dozen.**

Add a Decorative Touch

• Use traditional holiday cookie cutters, such as wreaths, trees, bells, or Santa. Or make your little ones proud by serving their friends cookies in shapes of airplanes, boats, clowns, or dinosaurs.
• Sprinkle cutout cookies with colored sugar or decorator candies before baking, or pipe red or green decorator frosting on cookies after they've cooled.

Rolled Christmas Cookies

1 cup butter or margarine, softened
1 cup sugar
2 large eggs
¼ cup milk
1½ teaspoons vanilla extract
3½ cups all-purpose flour
2 teaspoons baking powder
¾ teaspoon baking soda
¼ teaspoon ground cardamom
2 cups sifted powdered sugar
2 tablespoons lemon juice
2 tablespoons water
Paste food coloring
Assorted candies and decorations

Beat butter at medium speed of an electric mixer until creamy; gradually add sugar, beating well. Add eggs, one at a time, beating after each addition. Add milk and vanilla, and mix well.

Combine flour and next 3 ingredients; add to creamed mixture, stirring until blended. Shape dough into a ball; wrap in plastic wrap, and chill at least 2 hours.

Roll dough to ⅛-inch thickness on a well-floured surface; cut with shaped, 4-inch cookie cutters. Place on lightly greased cookie sheets.

Bake at 375° for 8 minutes or until edges are lightly browned. Cool on wire racks.

Combine powdered sugar, lemon juice, and water; tint glaze as desired with paste food coloring. Using a small, clean art brush, paint cookies as desired. Sprinkle with candy or decorations. **Yield: 6 dozen (4-inch) cookies.**

From top left: Ribbon Cookies, Christmas Bell Cookies, and Oatmeal-Nut-Chocolate Chip Cookies

Oatmeal-Nut-Chocolate Chip Cookies

1½ cups regular oats, uncooked
1 cup butter or margarine, softened
1 cup sugar
1 cup firmly packed brown sugar
2 large eggs
1 tablespoon vanilla extract
2 cups all-purpose flour
1 teaspoon baking soda
½ teaspoon baking powder
½ teaspoon salt
1 (12-ounce) package semisweet chocolate
   morsels
3 (1.5-ounce) bars milk chocolate, grated
1½ cups chopped pecans
12 ounces chocolate-flavored candy coating,
   melted (optional)

Place oats in container of an electric blender; process until finely ground. Set aside.

Beat butter in a large bowl at medium speed of an electric mixer until creamy; gradually add sugars, beating well. Add eggs and vanilla, mixing well.

Combine ground oats, flour, soda, baking powder, and salt; gradually add to creamed mixture, mixing well. Stir in chocolate morsels, grated chocolate, and pecans.

Drop dough by heaping teaspoonfuls onto greased cookie sheets. Bake at 375° for 10 to 12 minutes or until lightly browned. Cool slightly; remove to wire racks to cool completely.

Dip half of each cookie in candy coating, if desired; place on wax paper to cool. **Yield: about 9 dozen.**

Christmas Bell Cookies

⅔ cup butter or margarine, softened
¾ cup sugar
1 large egg
1 teaspoon grated orange rind
1 teaspoon vanilla extract
2 cups all-purpose flour
1½ teaspoons baking powder
30 maraschino cherries, halved

Beat butter at medium speed of an electric mixer until creamy; gradually add sugar, beating well. Add egg, orange rind, and vanilla; beat well.

Combine flour and baking powder; add to creamed mixture, beating until blended. Cover and chill 30 minutes.

Shape dough into two 8-inch rolls. Wrap rolls, and chill at least 8 hours.

Cut rolls into ¼-inch slices; place on ungreased cookie sheets. Place a cherry half on bottom half of each slice; fold in sides, overlapping and slightly covering cherry to resemble a bell.

Bake at 350° for 10 to 12 minutes. Cool on wire racks. **Yield: 5 dozen.**

Ribbon Cookies

1 cup butter or margarine, softened
1½ cups sugar
1 large egg
1 teaspoon vanilla extract
¼ teaspoon almond extract
2½ cups all-purpose flour
1½ teaspoons baking powder
½ teaspoon salt
½ cup finely chopped red candied cherries, divided
1 (1-ounce) square unsweetened chocolate, melted
¼ cup almonds

Line bottom and sides of a 9- x 5- x 3-inch loafpan with aluminum foil; set aside.

Beat butter at medium speed of an electric mixer until creamy; gradually add sugar, beating well. Add egg and flavorings; mix well.

Combine flour, baking powder, and salt. Add to creamed mixture; mix until blended.

Divide dough into thirds. Add half of cherries to one-third of dough; mix well. Press into pan. Knead chocolate and almonds into another third of dough; press over cherry layer. Add remaining cherries to remaining dough; press over chocolate layer. Cover and chill 8 hours.

Invert pan, and remove dough. Remove foil. Cut dough lengthwise into thirds. Cut each section of dough crosswise into ¼-inch slices. Place 1 inch apart on ungreased cookie sheets.

Bake at 350° for 10 to 12 minutes. Cool on wire racks. **Yield: about 7 dozen.**

Snowball Surprises

1 cup butter or margarine, softened
½ cup sugar
1 teaspoon vanilla extract
2 cups all-purpose flour
1 cup finely chopped pecans
10 chocolate-coated peppermint patties
Sifted powdered sugar

Beat butter at medium speed of an electric mixer until creamy; gradually add sugar, beating until light and fluffy. Stir in vanilla.

Stir in flour and pecans, mixing well; cover and chill at least 1 hour.

Cut peppermint patties into fourths. Press 1 tablespoon dough around each candy piece, forming a ball. Place on ungreased cookie sheets.

Bake at 350° for 12 minutes. (Cookies will not brown.) Cool 5 minutes on cookie sheets, and roll in powdered sugar. Place on wire racks to cool. **Yield: 40 cookies.**

Raspberry Brownies

½ cup butter or margarine, softened
1 cup sugar
2 large eggs
2 (1-ounce) squares unsweetened chocolate,
   melted
¾ cup all-purpose flour
1 cup chopped walnuts
⅓ cup raspberry jam

Beat butter at medium speed of an electric mixer until creamy; gradually add sugar, beating well.

Add eggs and chocolate to creamed mixture, mixing well. Add flour, mixing well; stir in walnuts.

Spoon half of batter into a greased and floured 9-inch square pan. Spread raspberry jam over batter; top with remaining batter. Bake at 350° for 28 to 30 minutes. Cut into squares. **Yield: 3 dozen.**

Macadamia-Oat Snowballs

1 cup butter or margarine, softened
½ cup sifted powdered sugar
1 teaspoon vanilla extract
2 cups all-purpose flour
¾ cup quick-cooking oats, uncooked
1 (3½-ounce) jar macadamia nuts, chopped
Powdered sugar

Beat butter at medium speed of an electric mixer until creamy; gradually add ½ cup powdered sugar, beating until light and fluffy.

Add vanilla and flour to creamed mixture, mixing well. Stir in oats and nuts. Shape into 1-inch balls; place on ungreased cookie sheets.

Bake at 375° for 12 minutes. Remove from pan; roll in powdered sugar, and cool on wire racks. **Yield: 4 dozen.**

Old-Fashioned Cutout Cookies

1 cup butter, softened
1 cup sifted powdered sugar
2¼ cups all-purpose flour
1 teaspoon vanilla extract
½ cup flaked coconut

Beat butter at medium speed of an electric mixer until creamy; gradually add sugar, beating well. Add flour and vanilla, mixing well.

Roll dough to ⅛-inch thickness on a lightly floured surface. Cut with a 3-inch lamb-shaped or other shaped cookie cutter; place on ungreased cookie sheets. Sprinkle with flaked coconut.

Bake at 375° for 7 to 9 minutes or until edges begin to brown. **Yield: 2 dozen.**

Molasses Crinkles

¾ cup shortening
1 cup firmly packed brown sugar
1 large egg
¼ cup molasses
2¼ cups all-purpose flour
2 teaspoons baking soda
½ teaspoon salt
1 teaspoon ground cinnamon
1 teaspoon ground ginger
½ teaspoon ground cloves
½ cup sugar

Beat shortening at medium speed of an electric mixer until fluffy; gradually add brown sugar, beating well. Add egg and molasses, mixing well.

Combine flour and next 5 ingredients. Add to creamed mixture; mix well. Cover; chill 2 hours.

Shape dough into 1-inch balls, and roll in sugar. Place 2 inches apart on lightly greased cookie sheets.

Bake at 350° for 12 to 15 minutes. Remove to wire racks to cool. **Yield: 4½ dozen.**

Clockwise from top left: Raspberry Brownies, Eggnog Logs (page 126), Old-Fashioned Cutout Cookies, Macadamia-Oat Snowballs, and Molasses Crinkles

Eggnog Logs

(pictured on page 125)

1 cup butter or margarine, softened
¾ cup sugar
1 large egg
2 teaspoons vanilla extract
1 teaspoon rum flavoring
3 cups all-purpose flour
1 teaspoon ground nutmeg
Vanilla Frosting
¾ cup chopped pecans, toasted

Beat butter at medium speed of an electric mixer until creamy; gradually add sugar, beating well. Add egg and flavorings, mixing well.

Combine flour and nutmeg; gradually add to creamed mixture, mixing well.

Divide dough into 10 portions. Roll each portion into a 15-inch-long rope, and cut each rope into 5 (3-inch) logs. Place 2 inches apart on ungreased cookie sheets.

Bake at 350° for 10 to 12 minutes. Cool on wire racks.

Dip log ends into Vanilla Frosting; roll in pecans. **Yield: 50 cookies.**

Vanilla Frosting

¼ cup butter or margarine, softened
2 cups sifted powdered sugar
2 tablespoons milk
1 teaspoon vanilla extract

Beat butter at medium speed of an electric mixer until creamy. Add sugar and milk alternately, beating after each addition. Add vanilla; beat until smooth and mixture reaches spreading consistency. **Yield: about 1 cup.**

Shortbread Cookies

¾ cup butter, softened
½ cup sugar
1 egg yolk
1½ cups all-purpose flour
½ teaspoon vanilla extract
Pecan halves

Beat butter at medium speed of an electric mixer until creamy; gradually add sugar, beating well. Add egg yolk, beating well. Add flour, mixing well. Stir in vanilla.

Shape dough into 1-inch balls, and place on ungreased cookie sheets. Gently press a pecan half in center of each cookie.

Bake at 300° for 14 to 16 minutes or until lightly browned. Cool 5 minutes; transfer to wire racks to cool completely. **Yield: 6 dozen.**

Tiny Christmas Bites

⅓ cup butter or margarine, melted
1 cup graham cracker crumbs
1 (14-ounce) can sweetened condensed milk
2 cups chopped pecans
1 cup chopped dates
1 (6-ounce) package frozen coconut, thawed
½ cup red candied cherries, chopped
½ cup candied pineapple, chopped
1 teaspoon vanilla extract
1 teaspoon almond extract

Combine butter and graham cracker crumbs; add sweetened condensed milk and remaining ingredients, stirring until blended.

Spoon 1 tablespoon into each cup of paper-lined miniature (1¾-inch) muffin pans.

Bake at 325° for 25 to 30 minutes. Remove from pans, and cool completely on wire racks. **Yield: 6 dozen.**

Clockwise from top: Shortbread Cookies, Christmas Tree Sandwich Cookies, and
Tiny Christmas Bites

Christmas Tree Sandwich Cookies

1¼ cups butter or margarine, softened
⅔ cup sugar
2 cups all-purpose flour
1 cup ground almonds
¾ cup ground hazelnuts, toasted
1 teaspoon ground cinnamon
⅔ cup seedless raspberry jam

Beat butter at medium speed of an electric mixer until fluffy; gradually add sugar, beating well. Gradually add flour, ground nuts, and cinnamon; beat at low speed just until dry ingredients are moistened. (Dough will be crumbly.)

Divide dough in half, and shape into a ball.

Wrap each portion, and chill at least 1 hour.

Roll one portion to ⅛-inch thickness on a lightly floured surface. Cut with a 3-inch tree-shaped cutter, and place on lightly greased cookie sheets.

Bake at 350° for 7 to 9 minutes or until lightly browned. Cool on wire racks.

Repeat procedure with remaining dough. Before baking, cut 4 or 5 small holes in each cookie, using a drinking straw. Bake as above, and cool on wire racks. Spread top of solid cookie with 1 teaspoon jam; top with cutout cookie.
Yield: 2½ dozen.

Clockwise from right: Raspberry-Filled Cookies, Chocolate-Hazelnut Sticks, and Cocoa Surprise Cookies (page 130)

Raspberry-Filled Cookies

1 cup butter, softened
½ cup sifted powdered sugar
2½ cups all-purpose flour
1 teaspoon vanilla extract
½ cup raspberry preserves

Beat butter at medium speed of an electric mixer until creamy; gradually add powdered sugar, beating until light and fluffy. Add flour and vanilla, mixing well. Shape dough into a ball.

Roll dough to ⅛-inch thickness on a lightly floured surface. Cut with a 2-inch round cutter. Use a ¾-inch cutter to cut out a flower or some other decorative design in center of half of cookies. Pierce solid cookies with the tines of a fork.

Place cookies on ungreased cookie sheets. Bake at 300° for 20 minutes or until cookies are very lightly browned. Cool on wire racks.

Spread top of each solid cookie with about ½ teaspoon raspberry preserves just before serving. Top each with cutout cookie. **Yield: 3 dozen.**

Chocolate-Hazelnut Sticks

⅔ cup whole hazelnuts or almonds
½ cup butter, softened
⅓ cup sugar
1 large egg
¾ teaspoon vanilla extract
1¼ cups all-purpose flour
Chocolate Glaze

Place hazelnuts on a baking sheet, and bake at 325° for 20 minutes, stirring occasionally. Cool 5 minutes; rub between hands to loosen skins; discard skins. Position knife blade in food processor bowl; add hazelnuts, and process until coarsely chopped. Set aside 3 tablespoons nuts for garnish, and finely grind remaining nuts.

Beat butter at medium speed of an electric mixer until creamy; gradually add sugar, beating well. Add egg and vanilla, beating until blended.

Add flour, beating until smooth. Fold in finely ground hazelnuts.

Use cookie gun fitted with a star-shaped disc to shape dough into decorative 2½-inch sticks, following manufacturer's directions. Place sticks on lightly greased cookie sheets.

Bake at 350° for 9 to 11 minutes or until lightly browned. Cool slightly on cookie sheets; remove to wire racks to cool completely.

Dip one end of each cookie in Chocolate Glaze, and sprinkle with reserved nuts. **Yield: 6 dozen.**

Chocolate Glaze

1 egg white
½ cup sifted powdered sugar
⅓ cup cocoa
⅛ teaspoon ground cinnamon
2 tablespoons butter, softened
2 tablespoons hot water
½ teaspoon vanilla extract

Beat egg white at medium speed of an electric mixer until frothy. Gradually add powdered sugar, cocoa, and cinnamon. Add butter, water, and vanilla, beating until blended. **Yield: ⅔ cup.**

Plan a Cookie Swap

- Have each guest bake a dozen or half-dozen cookies for each person attending, plus extras for sampling.
- Guests can package their cookies by the dozen or half-dozen for trading, or bring the whole batch in one container plus an empty container for collecting cookies from the other bakers.
- Ask guests to bring copies of their recipes.

Cocoa Surprise Cookies

(pictured on page 128)

1 cup butter or margarine, softened
⅔ cup sugar
1⅔ cups all-purpose flour
¼ cup cocoa
½ teaspoon vanilla extract
½ teaspoon chocolate menthe or mint
    flavoring
1 cup finely chopped pecans
1 (6-ounce) package crème de menthe
    wafers, unwrapped
1 cup sifted powdered sugar
1½ tablespoons milk
Few drops of green liquid food coloring

Beat butter at medium speed of an electric mixer until creamy; gradually add ⅔ cup sugar, beating well. Add flour and cocoa, mixing well. Stir in flavorings and pecans. Cover and chill 2 hours or until firm.

Shape dough into 36 balls. Shape each ball into an oval shape around each crème de menthe wafer. Place on ungreased cookie sheets, and chill 30 minutes.

Bake at 375° for 12 minutes. Cool slightly on cookie sheets; remove cookies to wire racks to cool completely.

Combine powdered sugar and milk, stirring until smooth; color with green food coloring. Place in a heavy-duty, zip-top plastic bag. Using scissors, snip a tiny hole in a bottom corner of bag; drizzle frosting over cookies. **Yield: 3 dozen.**

Double-Chocolate Cheesecake Squares

1¾ cups chocolate wafer crumbs
⅓ cup butter or margarine, melted
Vegetable cooking spray
4 (6-ounce) white chocolate-flavored baking
    bars, divided
2 (8-ounce) packages cream cheese, softened
½ cup sour cream
4 large eggs
2 teaspoons vanilla extract
¼ cup whipping cream
2 tablespoons Frangelico or other hazelnut
    liqueur

Combine chocolate wafer crumbs and melted butter; set aside 2 tablespoons. Press remaining crumb mixture in a 13- x 9- x 2-inch pan lined with heavy-duty aluminum foil coated with vegetable cooking spray.

Melt 16 ounces white chocolate baking bars in a heavy saucepan over low heat; cool slightly.

Beat cream cheese and sour cream at medium speed of an electric mixer until fluffy. Add eggs, one at a time, beating after each addition. Stir in vanilla and melted chocolate. Pour into prepared pan.

Bake at 300° for 30 minutes; turn oven off, and leave in oven 30 minutes. Cool on a wire rack.

Melt remaining 8 ounces white chocolate in a heavy saucepan over low heat. Remove from heat; stir in whipping cream and Frangelico. Pour over cheesecake, and sprinkle with reserved 2 tablespoons crumb mixture. Cover and chill at least 8 hours.

Lift cheesecake from pan, and remove foil. Cut into squares; place in individual paper baking cups to serve, if desired. **Yield: 4 dozen.**

Note: Cheesecake may be frozen up to 1 month in pan covered tightly with heavy-duty aluminum foil. To serve, remove frozen cheesecake from pan; thaw and cut into squares.

Double-Chocolate Cheesecake Squares

Sugar-Coated Chocolate Cookies

(pictured on page 109)

½ cup butter or margarine
3 (1-ounce) squares unsweetened chocolate
2 cups sugar
2 cups all-purpose flour
2 teaspoons baking powder
3 large eggs, lightly beaten
2 teaspoons vanilla extract
¾ cup sifted powdered sugar

Melt butter and chocolate in a heavy saucepan over low heat. Combine sugar, flour, and baking powder in a large bowl. Add chocolate mixture, eggs, and vanilla, mixing until smooth (mixture will be very thin). Cover and chill 2 hours.

Roll dough into 1-inch balls, and roll balls in powdered sugar. Place 2 inches apart on lightly greased cookie sheets.

Bake at 375° for 10 to 12 minutes. Remove to wire racks to cool. **Yield: 8 dozen.**

Cherry Crowns

(pictured on cover and page 109)

1 cup butter or margarine, softened
1 (3-ounce) package cream cheese, softened
1 cup sugar
1 large egg, separated
1 teaspoon almond extract
2½ cups all-purpose flour
1 cup finely ground blanched almonds
30 red candied cherries, halved

Beat butter and cream cheese at medium speed of an electric mixer until creamy; gradually add sugar, beating well.

Add egg yolk and almond extract, mixing well; gradually stir in flour. Cover; chill 1 hour.

Shape dough into 1-inch balls; dip tops of balls in lightly beaten egg white, and then in

almonds. Place 2 inches apart on lightly greased cookie sheets. Press a candied cherry half in center of each ball.

Bake at 350° for 15 minutes. Remove to wire racks to cool. **Yield: 5 dozen.**

Braided Candy Canes

(pictured on page 109)

¾ cup butter or margarine, softened
1 cup sugar
3 large eggs
1 tablespoon vanilla extract
4 cups all-purpose flour
1 tablespoon baking powder
½ teaspoon baking soda
1 egg white, lightly beaten
Red decorator sugar crystals

Beat butter at medium speed of an electric mixer until creamy; gradually add sugar, beating well. Add eggs and vanilla, mixing well.

Combine flour, baking powder, and soda; gradually add to creamed mixture, beating at low speed just until blended.

Divide dough into fourths. Divide each portion into 14 pieces, and roll each piece into a 9-inch rope. Fold each rope in half and twist. Shape twists into candy canes; brush with egg white, and sprinkle with sugar crystals.

Place cookies 2 inches apart on ungreased cookie sheets; bake at 350° for 15 minutes or until edges begin to brown. Remove to wire racks to cool. **Yield: 56 cookies.**

Note: These cookies can also be made into wreath shapes.

Chocolate-Mint Truffles

Chocolate-Mint Truffles

1 (12-ounce) package semisweet chocolate
   morsels
4 egg yolks
⅓ cup butter or margarine, cut into pieces
⅓ cup sifted powdered sugar
½ teaspoon mint extract
16 ounces chocolate-flavored candy coating
4 ounces vanilla-flavored candy coating,
   melted

Place chocolate morsels in top of a double boiler; bring water to a boil. Reduce heat to low; cook until chocolate melts, stirring often. Remove top of double boiler from hot water.

Beat yolks until thick and pale. Stir about one-fourth of melted chocolate into yolks; add to remaining melted chocolate, stirring constantly.

Place top of double boiler over boiling water, and cook 2 minutes. Remove top of double boiler from hot water, and add butter, sugar, and mint extract; beat at medium speed of a hand-held electric mixer until butter melts and mixture is smooth. Cover with paper towel, and let stand in a cool, dry place 1 hour (do not refrigerate).

Shape mixture into ¾-inch balls; chill 1 hour.

Place chocolate-flavored candy coating in top of double boiler; bring water to a boil. Reduce heat to low; cook until coating melts. Remove from heat, leaving top of double boiler over hot water. Dip each ball into candy coating, letting excess coating drip off. Place on wax paper-lined cookie sheets, and chill until coating hardens. Drizzle truffles with melted vanilla-flavored candy coating. **Yield: 4 dozen.**

Strawberry Fudge Balls

Strawberry Fudge Balls

1 (8-ounce) package cream cheese, softened
1 (6-ounce) package semisweet chocolate
   morsels, melted
¾ cup vanilla wafer crumbs
¼ cup strawberry preserves
½ cup almonds, toasted and finely chopped
Powdered Sugar

Beat cream cheese at medium speed of an electric mixer until fluffy. Add melted chocolate, beating until smooth. Stir in wafer crumbs and preserves; cover and chill 1 hour.

Shape mixture into 1-inch balls; roll in almonds or powdered sugar. Store in an airtight container in refrigerator, or freeze up to 2 months. **Yield: 4 dozen.**

Variation

Raspberry Fudge Balls: Substitute ¼ cup red raspberry jam for strawberry preserves and ⅔ cup ground pecans, toasted, for ½ cup almonds.

Coconut Shortbread Cookies

¾ cup butter or margarine, softened
⅓ cup sugar
1½ teaspoons vanilla extract
1¾ cups all-purpose flour
½ teaspoon baking powder
¼ teaspoon salt
1 cup flaked coconut
1 (6-ounce) package semisweet chocolate
   morsels
2 teaspoons shortening
Flaked coconut, toasted

Beat butter at medium speed of an electric mixer until creamy; gradually add sugar, beating until light and fluffy. Stir in vanilla.

Combine flour, baking powder, and salt; gradually add to creamed mixture, mixing well. Stir in 1 cup coconut. Cover and chill 1 hour.

Roll dough to ¼-inch thickness on a lightly floured surface. Cut dough into desired shapes with 2-inch cookie cutters, and place on lightly greased cookie sheets.

Bake at 300° for 25 to 30 minutes or until edges are lightly browned. Remove to wire racks to cool.

Melt chocolate morsels and shortening in a small, heavy saucepan over low heat. Dip edges of cookies in chocolate mixture; then dip in toasted coconut. Place on cookie sheets lined with wax paper. Chill 10 minutes. **Yield: 2 dozen.**

Christmas Trees

(pictured on page 137)

1½ cups butter or margarine, softened
1 cup sugar
1 (3-ounce) package lime-flavored gelatin
1 large egg
1 teaspoon vanilla extract
4 cups all-purpose flour
1 teaspoon baking powder
Red and green sugar crystals (optional)

Beat butter at medium speed of an electric mixer until creamy; add sugar and gelatin, beating well. Add egg and vanilla; beat well.

Combine flour and baking powder; add to creamed mixture, and mix well.

Use a cookie gun to shape dough as desired, following the manufacturer's instructions. Place cookies on ungreased cookie sheets; decorate with sugar crystals, if desired.

Bake at 350° for 12 to 15 minutes. Cool on wire racks. **Yield: about 9½ dozen.**

Frosted Chocolate-Cherry Cookies

1½ cups butter or margarine, softened
1½ cups sugar
2 large eggs
1 tablespoon vanilla extract
3¼ cups all-purpose flour
½ teaspoon baking powder
½ teaspoon baking soda
¼ teaspoon salt
⅔ cup cocoa
1 (10-ounce) jar maraschino cherries
Chocolate-Cherry Frosting

Beat butter at medium speed of an electric mixer until creamy; gradually add sugar, beating well. Add eggs and vanilla; beat well.

Combine flour and next 4 ingredients; add to creamed mixture, and mix well.

Shape dough into 1-inch balls; place about 2 inches apart on ungreased cookie sheets. Press thumb in center of cookie, leaving an indentation. Drain cherries, reserving juice. Cut cherries in half, and place, cut side down, in indentation of cookie.

Bake at 350° for 8 minutes. Cool; drizzle with Chocolate-Cherry Frosting. **Yield: 6 dozen.**

Chocolate-Cherry Frosting

1 (1-ounce) square unsweetened chocolate
1 tablespoon butter or margarine
1 cup sifted powdered sugar
5 to 6 tablespoons cherry juice

Melt chocolate and butter in a heavy saucepan over low heat, stirring constantly. Remove from heat. Add powdered sugar and half of cherry juice; beat until mixture is smooth. Add juice to desired consistency; stir well. **Yield: ¾ cup.**

Note: Cookies may be frozen up to 1 week. Place in single layers in heavy-duty, zip-top plastic bags.

Orange Slice Cookies

1½ cups chopped candy orange slices
¼ cup all-purpose flour
1 cup butter or margarine, softened
1 cup firmly packed brown sugar
¾ cup sugar
2 large eggs
2 tablespoons milk
2 tablespoons vanilla extract
2 cups all-purpose flour
1 teaspoon baking soda
½ teaspoon salt
½ teaspoon ground cinnamon
½ teaspoon ground nutmeg
2½ cups quick-cooking oats, uncooked
1 cup flaked coconut

Combine orange slices and ¼ cup flour in a medium bowl; toss to coat candy. Set aside.

Beat butter at medium speed of an electric mixer until creamy; gradually add sugars, beating well. Add eggs, milk, and vanilla; beat well.

Combine 2 cups flour and next 4 ingredients; gradually add to creamed mixture, beating well. Stir in candy mixture, oats, and coconut.

Drop dough by rounded teaspoonfuls 2 inches apart onto greased cookie sheets.

Bake at 375° for 10 minutes. Cool slightly on cookie sheets; remove to wire racks. **Yield: 9 dozen.**

Holiday Packaging Ideas

• Check stores for tins, bags, baskets, and boxes. Line with colorful napkins, plastic wrap, or tissue.
• Decorate small paper bags with stencils or rubber stamps and ink. Trim top of bags with pinking shears. Fold down top; seal with stickers, or weave ribbon through holes punched in bag to close.

Orange Slice Cookies, Frosted Chocolate-Cherry Cookies, and Christmas Trees (page 135)

Clockwise from top: Chocolate-Dipped Orange Logs (page 140), Cookie Wreaths, and Chocolate-Peppermint Cups

Chocolate-Peppermint Cups

1 cup whipping cream
⅛ teaspoon cream of tartar
2 cups sugar
2 drops of peppermint oil
1 or 2 drops of red or green liquid food
    coloring
3 to 4 ounces chocolate-flavored candy coating
Crushed peppermint candy

Combine first 3 ingredients in a saucepan; stir gently. Bring to a boil, without stirring. Cook, without stirring, until mixture reaches soft ball stage (236°). Remove from heat.

Rinse a 12- x 8- x 2-inch baking dish with cold water, and immediately pour cooked mixture into dish. Cool to lukewarm (about 105°). Using a wooden spoon, work mixture back and forth until mixture is creamy white and begins to harden. Cover with damp cloth; let stand 5 minutes.

Knead fondant mixture by hand until soft and creamy, kneading in peppermint oil. (Mixture may become warmer and thinner just before ready.) Place fondant in a plastic bag for at least 1 hour.

Place fondant in top of a double boiler; bring water to a boil. Reduce heat to low; cook over hot water until mixture reaches 170°. Stir in food coloring. Let mixture cool to the touch, and shape into ¾-inch balls. Press each ball into a 1-inch foil cup.

Melt candy coating in a heavy saucepan over low heat. Spoon a thin layer of melted coating into each cup of fondant. Sprinkle with crushed peppermint candy; cool. Remove foil cups before serving. **Yield: 2½ dozen.**

Cookie Wreaths

2½ cups all-purpose flour
¼ teaspoon salt
¾ cup sugar
2 teaspoons grated orange rind
1 cup butter or margarine
¼ cup orange juice
1 egg white, beaten
1 teaspoon water
¼ cup sugar
⅓ cup ground almonds
1 teaspoon grated orange rind
Tube of green decorator frosting
Red cinnamon candies

Combine first 4 ingredients; cut in butter with a pastry blender until mixture is crumbly.

Sprinkle orange juice evenly over surface; stir mixture with a fork until dry ingredients are moistened. Shape dough into a ball; cover and chill.

Work with half of dough at a time, and store remainder in refrigerator. Divide first portion of dough into 48 balls. Roll 2 balls into 5-inch ropes. Place ropes on a lightly greased cookie sheet; pinch ends together at one end to seal. Twist ropes together, and shape strip into a circle, pinching ends to seal.

Repeat procedure with remaining 46 balls and other portion of dough. Combine egg white and water; brush over cookies.

Combine ¼ cup sugar, almonds, and 1 teaspoon orange rind; sprinkle mixture on cookies. Bake at 400° for 8 to 10 minutes or until browned. Cool on wire racks.

Pipe holly leaves with green frosting, and top with cinnamon candies. **Yield: 4 dozen.**

Chocolate-Rum Balls

Chocolate-Dipped Orange Logs

(pictured on page 138)

1 cup butter or margarine, softened
½ cup sifted powdered sugar
1 teaspoon grated orange rind
1 teaspoon orange extract
2 cups all-purpose flour
6 ounces chocolate-flavored candy coating
½ cup chopped almonds, toasted

Beat butter at medium speed of an electric mixer until creamy; gradually add sugar, beating until light and fluffy. Stir in orange rind and extract. Gradually add flour to creamed mixture; mix well.

Shape dough into 2½- x ½-inch logs. Place on ungreased cookie sheets. Using a fork, flatten three-fourths of each cookie lengthwise to ¼-inch thickness.

Bake at 350° for 11 minutes. Transfer to wire racks to cool.

Melt chocolate coating in a heavy saucepan over low heat, stirring occasionally. Dip unflattened tips of cookies in melted coating to coat both sides; roll coated portion in almonds. Place cookies on wire racks until coating is firm.

Arrange cookies between layers of wax paper in an airtight container. **Yield: 4 dozen.**

Chocolate-Rum Balls

1 (9-ounce) package chocolate wafer cookies, crushed
1 cup chopped pecans
1 cup sifted powdered sugar
¼ cup light corn syrup
¼ cup dark rum
Additional powdered sugar

Combine first 5 ingredients in a large bowl; stir well. Shape into 1-inch balls, and let stand 10 minutes. Sprinkle additional powdered sugar over balls. **Yield: 4 dozen.**

Index